Alphabet Soup

Expressive Quilts with Folk-Art Charm

Tammy Johnson
& Avis Shirer

Martingale®
& C O M P A N Y

Acknowledgments

We would like to thank Deb McGaugh of Sew What Quilting for the wonderful machine quilting she did on these projects. She brought these quilts to life with her amazing vision and imagination. We truly appreciate her work. And thanks to our family and friends for supporting us during this wonderful adventure.

Alphabet Soup: Expressive Quilts with Folk-Art Charm
© 2005 by Tammy Johnson and Avis Shirer

That Patchwork Place® is an imprint
of Martingale & Company®.

Martingale & Company
20205 144th Avenue NE
Woodinville, WA 98072-8478 USA
www.martingale-pub.com

Printed in China
10 09 08 07 06 05   8 7 6 5 4 3 2 1

Library of Congress Cataloging-in-Publication Data

Johnson, Tammy.

  Alphabet soup / Tammy Johnson and Avis Shirer.

    p. cm.

  ISBN 1-56477-621-2

  1. Appliqué—Patterns. 2. Quilts. 3. Quilting.
4. Alphabet in art. I. Shirer, Avis. II. Title.

  TT779.S51732 2005

  746.44'5041—dc22

                      2005008699

Credits

President ✦ Nancy J. Martin

CEO ✦ Daniel J. Martin

VP and General Manager ✦ Tom Wierzbicki

Publisher ✦ Jane Hamada

Editorial Director ✦ Mary V. Green

Managing Editor ✦ Tina Cook

Technical Editor ✦ Karen Costello Soltys

Copy Editor ✦ Sheila Chapman Ryan

Design Director ✦ Stan Green

Illustrator ✦ Laurel Strand

Cover and Text Designer ✦ Regina Girard

Photographer ✦ Brent Kane

Mission Statement
Dedicated to providing quality products
and service to inspire creativity.

Contents

Introduction

Remember sitting at the kitchen table with a warm bowl of alphabet soup? Tammy and I have fond memories of fishing around in the soup with our spoons, hunting for the right letters, and scooping them up one at a time until the spoon held the letters for "dog" or "cat" or our names.

This book will help you to bring some of those memories back to life in quilting projects. The quilts are based on some of our favorite things: baskets, flowers, pumpkins, and home, to name a few. We had such fun designing and sewing the quilts for this book. They have a primitive flair that both the beginner and more experienced quilter will enjoy. Piecing the letters is a bit like putting together a puzzle; at first the task seems large, but once a few pieces of the puzzle are assembled, it becomes child's play. And don't be intimidated if you don't appliqué. We primarily use

fusible appliqué embellished with a machine blanket stitch. Of course, you could appliqué by hand if you prefer.

Because the letters are used in all the quilts, we decided to give the cutting and piecing instructions for each letter only once, rather than take up lots of room repeating instructions. Each specific project will tell you how much letter fabric and background fabric you need, and which letters you need to piece. Then you'll need to turn to "The Alphabet" on page 11 for cutting and piecing directions for the letters. The rest of the cutting and piecing instructions for sewing the letters together, as well as for assembling the rest of the quilt, are with the project instructions.

Tammy and I enjoy collecting fabrics, and we always end up visiting a quilt shop or two when we travel together. We often buy exactly the same fabrics,

Avis and Tammy

but generally tend to use them differently. When we purchase fabric, we normally do not have a project in mind; we just purchase with our hearts—and with an eye for color. That's what enables us to incorporate a large variety of fabrics into each project, with homespun plaids and stripes being our favorites. Putting together unexpected color combinations adds a bit of whimsy to our folk-art designs. And we don't stop with color. We love to combine flannels with wovens, and often embellish with velveteen, wool, buttons, or rickrack.

Our favorite quilts are seasonal ones. We both grew up in rural, northern Iowa where we had four distinct seasons. Tammy enjoys winter much more than I do. She loves Christmas, and snowmen are her favorite. I, on the other hand, adore Halloween as well as anything with flowers. Our partnership is so fortunate that we enjoy different seasonal themes; that way the entire year is covered!

When we design, we always design from our hearts. Our designs come from something that we remember as a child or a special memory in our lives. We look at a flower or a tree or even some of the

wonderful colors in nature and are inspired to create a new quilting project.

People often ask how we came to name our business Joined at the Hip. The answer is really very simple. We are two friends that thoroughly enjoy each other's company, so much so that our husbands call each other wanting to know where we are. They always say we are joined at the hip. We thought that was true and rather catchy, and thus the name of our company. Our taste is so similar in quilting, design, and color that most people cannot determine which one of us has designed the projects. In fact, our taste is so much alike that we will unknowingly purchase the same clothes. Before we go to any event where we will be together, we do a "what are you wearing?" check!

It is our hope that you will enjoy the projects in *Alphabet Soup*. We had a delightful time creating them. Quilting is something that comes from the heart and soul. We hope these projects warm your heart and soul—just like soup. Enjoy!

Avis Shirer
Joined at the Hip

Appliqué and Quiltmaking Basics

The techniques we use to make our quilts include basic rotary cutting, some shortcut piecing, and fusible appliqué that we like to finish with machine blanket-stitching for a decorative touch. You may be familiar with all of these techniques already, but if you need some guidance, we've covered the basics for you in this section.

Supplies

Rotary-cutting tools: You will need a cutting mat, rotary cutter, and clear acrylic rulers to complete the projects in this book. Rulers come in many shapes and sizes. A 6" x 24" long ruler and a 12½" square ruler are good sizes to start with.

Sewing machine: A sewing machine in good working order is a must-have. The majority of stitching is done with a straight stitch. We use the machine blanket stitch to finish the edges of fused appliqués. If you plan to machine quilt your projects as we've done, you will find a walking foot and a darning foot very helpful.

Fusible web: If you want to stitch around the edges of the fused appliqués, make sure to use a lightweight fusible web.

Tracing fabric: We use this product for invisible machine appliqué. It is a lightweight fabric, similar to interfacing, that is used in dressmaking to trace clothing patterns. It is usually marked with a grid or dots.

Batting: While there are many types of batting available, we used cotton batting for all of the quilts in this book. Cotton batting gives a very flat look, and if the finished quilt is washed, it will take on the look of a crinkled antique quilt.

Rotary Cutting

Rotary cutting will make the process of constructing a quilt much more accurate and much faster than cutting the pieces with scissors. The following steps will guide you in the process.

1. Fold the fabric with the selvages together. Lay the fabric on the cutting mat with the fold toward you, aligning the fabric on a horizontal line on the mat.

2. Lay a small square ruler along the folded edge of the fabric, aligning a line on the ruler with the folded edge of the fabric. Then lay a long ruler to the left of the square ruler so that the edges touch.

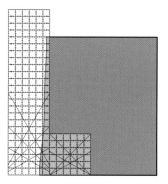

3. Remove the square ruler, keeping the long ruler in place. Cut along the right edge of the long ruler with a rotary cutter. The edge of the fabric is now straight and ready for you to cut your strips.

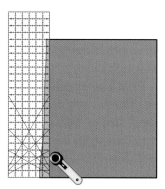

4. Line up the straight edge of the fabric with the line on the ruler that corresponds with the required measurement. Cut the strip.

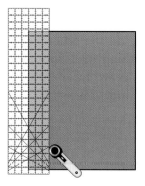

5. Trim the selvages off the ends of the strip. Line up the left side of the strip with the correct ruler line. Cut along the right edge of the ruler.

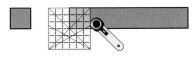

6. To cut a half-square triangle, cut a square the size indicated in the cutting directions. Lay a ruler across the square diagonally and cut from corner to corner. One square will yield two half-square triangles.

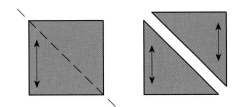

Folded Corners

One piecing shortcut we use often to make the letter blocks in our quilts is the folded-corner technique. It makes quick work of adding diagonal corners to squares and rectangles and gives neat and accurate results. The block instructions will give the sizes to cut each piece. The following steps explain how to do the piecing.

1. Fold the square that will be used to make the corner in half diagonally and crease it to mark the stitching line. Or, use a pencil and ruler to draw a diagonal line from corner to corner on the wrong side of the square.

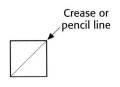

Crease or pencil line

2. Place the square right sides together with the strip, rectangle, or larger square as shown in the project illustration. Make sure the diagonal line is pointing in the correct direction, and then stitch on the creased or drawn stitching line.

Stitch.

3. Trim away the outer corner of the square, cutting ¼" from the stitching line. Leave the bottom layer (square, rectangle, or strip) intact. This will help stabilize the corner. Flip open the top square of fabric and press to complete the folded corner.

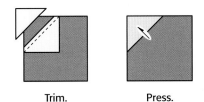

Trim.   Press.

Appliqué

We generally use fusible appliqué because it's fast and easy, making this collection of small quilts a snap to complete. However, for really large shapes, we prefer not to use fusible web as it can make a quilt too stiff. In that case, we use invisible machine appliqué. Both techniques are described below.

Fusible Appliqué

1. For this technique the templates need to be reversed from the image shown in the completed quilt. In this book, we've already reversed the patterns for you. Simply trace the patterns from the book pages onto template plastic and cut them out on the drawn lines.

2. Trace the template onto the paper side of the fusible-web material.

Fusible web (paper side up)

3. Cut out the shape, cutting about ¼" *outside* of the traced line. Do not cut on the line!

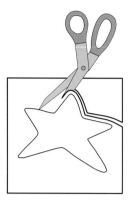

4. Place the fusible-web material, traced side up, on the wrong side of the appropriate fabric. Use your iron to press the fusible web onto the fabric following the manufacturer's directions. Cut out the shape along the traced line. Remove the paper backing.

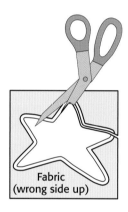

Fabric
(wrong side up)

5. Place the template with the shiny adhesive side down on the right side of the background fabric and press in place.

6. Finish the edges of the appliqués by stitching around them with a decorative stitch. We used a machine blanket stitch for most of the appliqués in this book.

Invisible Machine Appliqué

For this technique, the templates *do not* need to be reversed.

1. Trace the template shape onto lightweight tracing fabric (see "Supplies" on page 6). Cut out the shape approximately ¼" outside of the traced line.

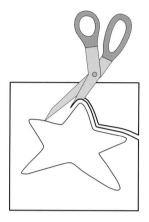

2. Lay the tracing fabric on the right side of the appropriate fabric with the traced side up.

3. Stitching on the marked line, machine stitch all the way around the shape. Begin and end in the same place; do not leave an opening for turning the shape right side out.

Tracing fabric
(traced
side up)

Fabric
(right side up)

4. Cut out the shape ⅛" to ¼" outside of the sewn line. Make a slit in the tracing material only. Turn right side out through the opening.

5. Position the appliqué onto the right side of the background fabric. Thread your sewing machine with a thread that blends with the color of the background fabric. Set your machine to a blind hem stitch. You will need to adjust the stitch length and width to a very short and narrow stitch. Using thread that blends with the background fabric, stitch on the background fabric along the edge of the shape. The machine will stitch about five straight stitches and then jump over to catch the shape. This stitch should just catch the edge of the appliqué. You may want to practice on some scrap fabric to get the stitch length and width you desire. The result is nearly invisible, imitating the look of hand appliqué.

Making Bias Vines

We have used bias strips to make the vine appliqués in some of the projects in this book. We like to use bias bars to make this task easier and more accurate. Bias bars are available at your local quilt shop. Make these strips as follows:

1. Use a rotary cutter, a mat, and an acrylic ruler to cut a strip of vine fabric *on the bias*. For the vines in this book, we cut the strips 1⅜" wide.

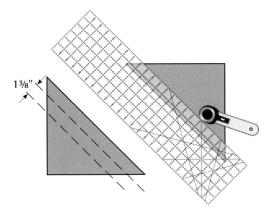

2. Stitch the strips together end to end to create the desired length of bias.

3. Fold the strip in half lengthwise, wrong sides together, and stitch ⅛" from the long raw edge.

4. Slide the appropriate-sized bias bar into the tube, manipulating the fabric until the seam is centered along one side of the bar. Press well, pressing the seam allowance to one side. Continue moving the bar and pressing for the entire length of the tube. Remove the bias bar and press again.

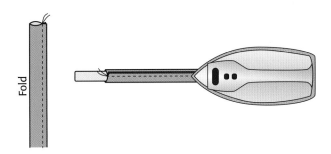

5. Cut the bias strip into the lengths specified. Position them onto the background fabric according to the project directions and stitch them in place by machine using a blind hem stitch. Shorten the stitch width and length. Stitch close to the edge of the strip onto the background fabric. The needle will jump over to catch the strip every four or five stitches. You may want to practice on a fabric scrap first.

Quilting and Binding

1. When the quilt top is done, make a "sandwich" by layering the backing fabric, batting, and quilt top. The batting and backing pieces are cut 6" larger than the quilt top. Lay the backing fabric face down on a flat surface. Secure the edges with masking tape to keep the back smooth.

2. Lay the batting piece on top of the backing. Smooth out all the wrinkles, and then center the quilt top face up over the batting.

3. Baste the sandwich using a needle and thread, safety pins, or basting spray.

4. Quilt as desired by hand or machine. The quilts in this book were machine quilted.

5. We like to use single-fold binding to finish the quilt edges. Cut 1½"-wide strips across the width of the binding fabric to make single-fold binding. Join the strips (as shown in "Making Bias Vines" on page 9) to make one strip long enough to go all the way around the quilt plus at least 10" for turning the corners and finishing the ends.

6. Stitch the binding in place on the right side of the quilt top through all the layers, raw edges aligned, using a ¼" seam allowance. Start at the middle of the lower edge of the quilt. Start stitching 1" from the end of the binding strip. Stop stitching ¼" from the corner of the quilt. Backstitch and cut the thread.

7. Turn the quilt so you can sew down the next side. Fold the binding strip up, forming a 45° angle. Bring the binding strip down on itself. Stitch along the edge, again using a ¼" seam allowance.

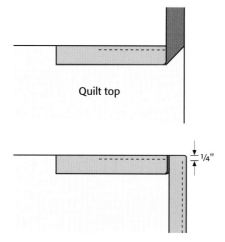

Quilt top

¼"

8. Repeat this process for each corner. When you are close to the beginning of the binding, fold back the 1" tail that was left at the start of the binding. Then overlap the other end of the binding with the 1" folded edge, and continue stitching to hold all three layers in place. Trim away any excess binding.

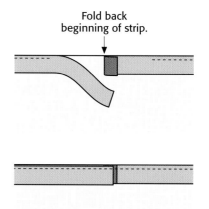

Fold back beginning of strip.

9. Using a long ruler and rotary cutter, trim the batting and backing even with the edge of the quilt top. Fold the binding over the raw edge of the quilt. Hand stitch the binding in place using a blind stitch, turning under ¼" on the raw edge of the binding strip as you go.

Quilt back

The Alphabet

Each letter of the alphabet has its own set of cutting directions called the "Cutting Recipe." It states the size of each piece to be cut from the letter fabric and the background fabric. For the specific colors and letters needed for your project, refer to the materials list and project directions for the quilt you are making.

A series of illustrations show how to assemble each letter. Sometimes the folded-corner technique (page 7) is used to shape parts of the letter before the letter is assembled.

A

Cutting Recipe

From the letter fabric, cut:
A: 2 pieces, 1½" x 6½"
B: 2 pieces, 1½" x 2½"
C: 2 squares, 1½" x 1½"

From the background fabric, cut:
D: 1 piece, 2½" x 3½"
E: 1 square, 2½" x 2½"
F: 6 squares, 1½" x 1½"

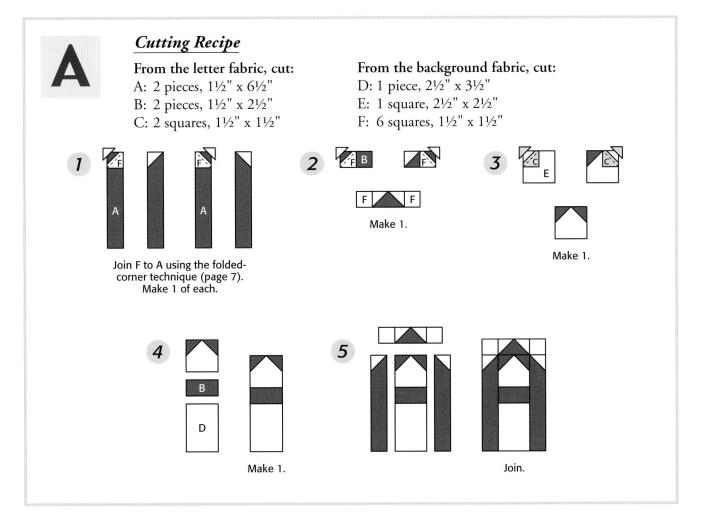

1
Join F to A using the folded-corner technique (page 7).
Make 1 of each.

2
Make 1.

3
Make 1.

4
Make 1.

5
Join.

11

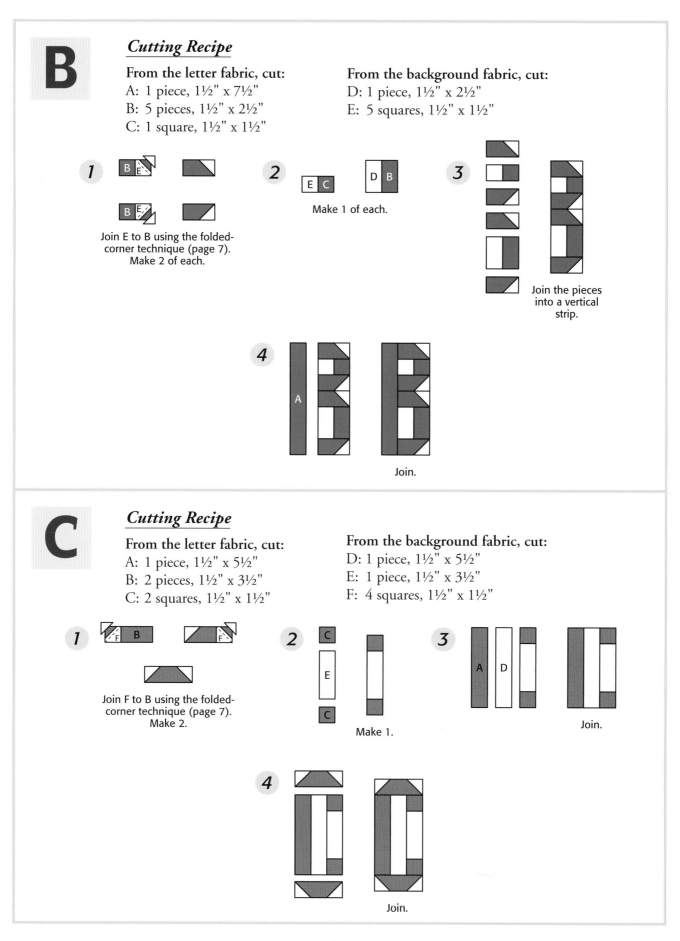

B

Cutting Recipe

From the letter fabric, cut:
A: 1 piece, 1½" x 7½"
B: 5 pieces, 1½" x 2½"
C: 1 square, 1½" x 1½"

From the background fabric, cut:
D: 1 piece, 1½" x 2½"
E: 5 squares, 1½" x 1½"

1

Join E to B using the folded-corner technique (page 7).
Make 2 of each.

2

Make 1 of each.

3

Join the pieces into a vertical strip.

4

Join.

C

Cutting Recipe

From the letter fabric, cut:
A: 1 piece, 1½" x 5½"
B: 2 pieces, 1½" x 3½"
C: 2 squares, 1½" x 1½"

From the background fabric, cut:
D: 1 piece, 1½" x 5½"
E: 1 piece, 1½" x 3½"
F: 4 squares, 1½" x 1½"

1

Join F to B using the folded-corner technique (page 7).
Make 2.

2

Make 1.

3

Join.

4

Join.

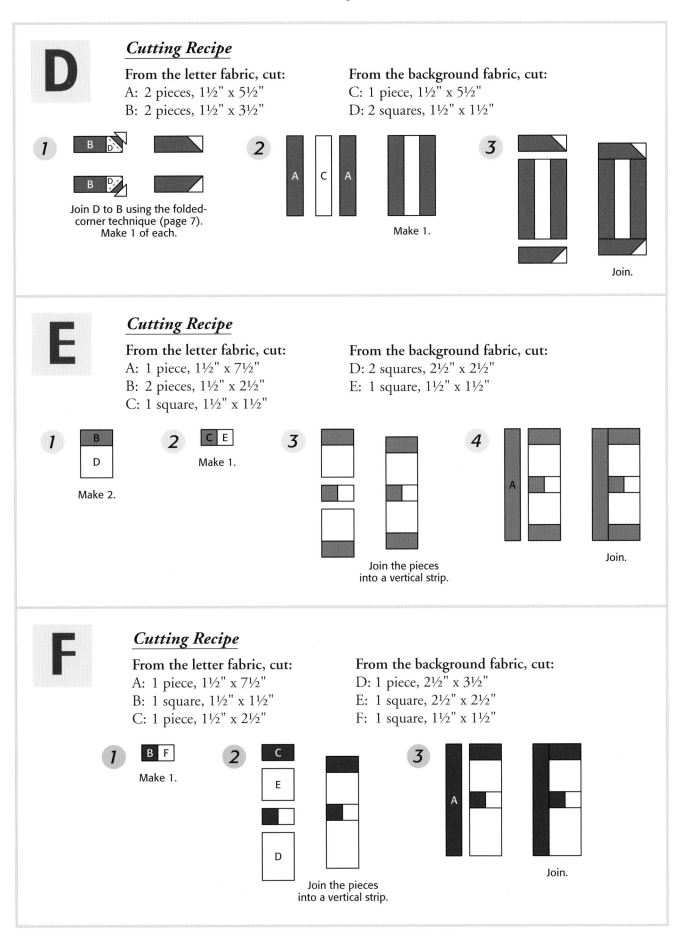

D

Cutting Recipe

From the letter fabric, cut:
A: 2 pieces, 1½" x 5½"
B: 2 pieces, 1½" x 3½"

From the background fabric, cut:
C: 1 piece, 1½" x 5½"
D: 2 squares, 1½" x 1½"

1 Join D to B using the folded-corner technique (page 7). Make 1 of each.

2 Make 1.

3 Join.

E

Cutting Recipe

From the letter fabric, cut:
A: 1 piece, 1½" x 7½"
B: 2 pieces, 1½" x 2½"
C: 1 square, 1½" x 1½"

From the background fabric, cut:
D: 2 squares, 2½" x 2½"
E: 1 square, 1½" x 1½"

1 Make 2.

2 Make 1.

3 Join the pieces into a vertical strip.

4 Join.

F

Cutting Recipe

From the letter fabric, cut:
A: 1 piece, 1½" x 7½"
B: 1 square, 1½" x 1½"
C: 1 piece, 1½" x 2½"

From the background fabric, cut:
D: 1 piece, 2½" x 3½"
E: 1 square, 2½" x 2½"
F: 1 square, 1½" x 1½"

1 Make 1.

2 Join the pieces into a vertical strip.

3 Join.

G

Cutting Recipe

From the letter fabric, cut:
A: 1 piece, 1½" x 5½"
B: 2 pieces, 1½" x 4½"
C: 1 piece, 1½" x 2½"
D: 2 squares, 1½" x 1½"

From the background fabric, cut:
E: 1 piece, 2½" x 3½"
F: 2 pieces, 1½" x 2½"
G: 5 squares, 1½" x 1½"

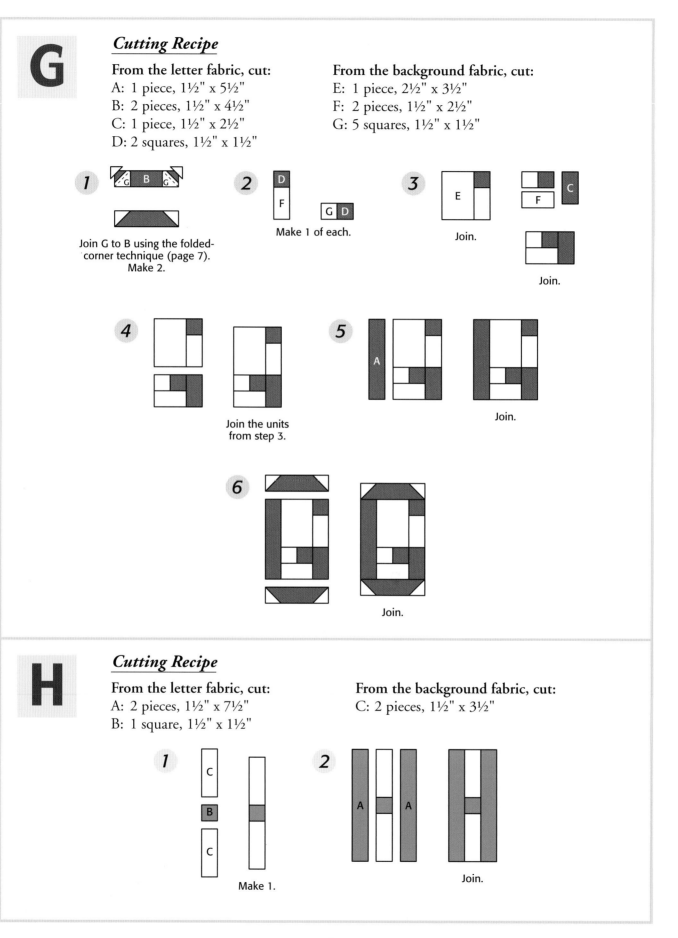

1 Join G to B using the folded-corner technique (page 7). Make 2.

2 Make 1 of each.

3 Join. / Join.

4 Join the units from step 3.

5 Join.

6 Join.

H

Cutting Recipe

From the letter fabric, cut:
A: 2 pieces, 1½" x 7½"
B: 1 square, 1½" x 1½"

From the background fabric, cut:
C: 2 pieces, 1½" x 3½"

1 Make 1.

2 Join.

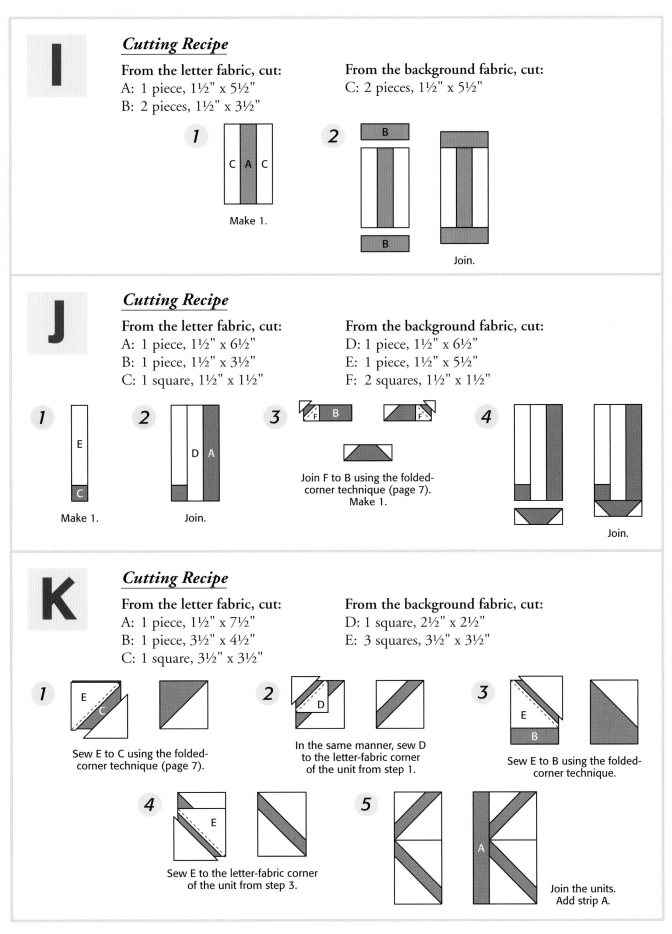

I

Cutting Recipe

From the letter fabric, cut:
A: 1 piece, 1½" x 5½"
B: 2 pieces, 1½" x 3½"

From the background fabric, cut:
C: 2 pieces, 1½" x 5½"

1 C A C
Make 1.

2 B / B Join.

J

Cutting Recipe

From the letter fabric, cut:
A: 1 piece, 1½" x 6½"
B: 1 piece, 1½" x 3½"
C: 1 square, 1½" x 1½"

From the background fabric, cut:
D: 1 piece, 1½" x 6½"
E: 1 piece, 1½" x 5½"
F: 2 squares, 1½" x 1½"

1 E C
Make 1.

2 D A
Join.

3 F B / F
Join F to B using the folded-corner technique (page 7).
Make 1.

4 Join.

K

Cutting Recipe

From the letter fabric, cut:
A: 1 piece, 1½" x 7½"
B: 1 piece, 3½" x 4½"
C: 1 square, 3½" x 3½"

From the background fabric, cut:
D: 1 square, 2½" x 2½"
E: 3 squares, 3½" x 3½"

1 E C
Sew E to C using the folded-corner technique (page 7).

2 D
In the same manner, sew D to the letter-fabric corner of the unit from step 1.

3 E B
Sew E to B using the folded-corner technique.

4 E
Sew E to the letter-fabric corner of the unit from step 3.

5 A
Join the units.
Add strip A.

L

Cutting Recipe

From the letter fabric, cut:
A: 1 piece, 1½" x 7½"
B: 1 piece, 1½" x 2½"

From the background fabric, cut:
C: 1 piece, 2½" x 6½"

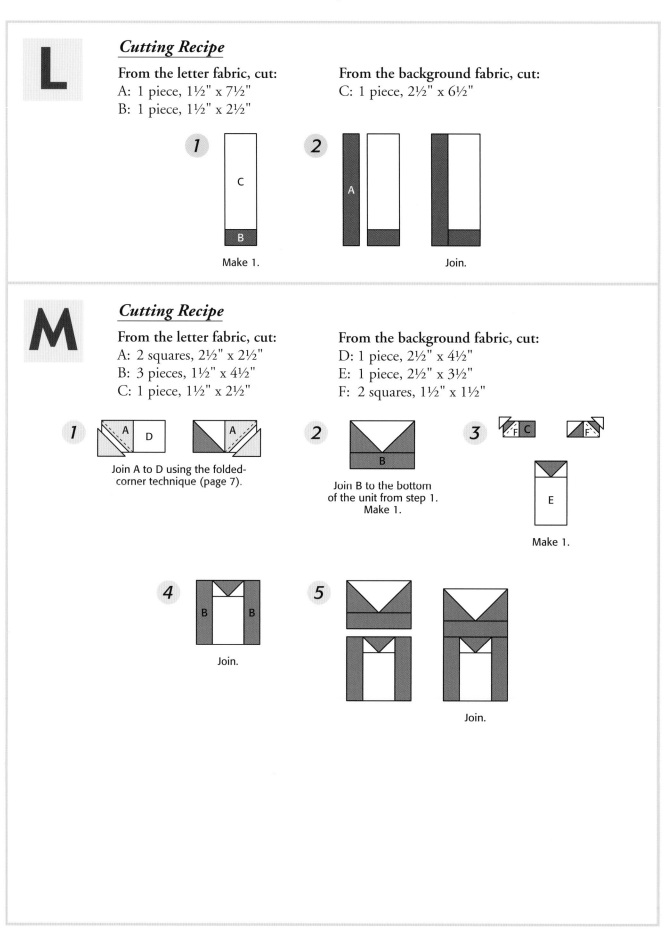

1 Make 1.

2 Join.

M

Cutting Recipe

From the letter fabric, cut:
A: 2 squares, 2½" x 2½"
B: 3 pieces, 1½" x 4½"
C: 1 piece, 1½" x 2½"

From the background fabric, cut:
D: 1 piece, 2½" x 4½"
E: 1 piece, 2½" x 3½"
F: 2 squares, 1½" x 1½"

1 Join A to D using the folded-corner technique (page 7).

2 Join B to the bottom of the unit from step 1. Make 1.

3 Make 1.

4 Join.

5 Join.

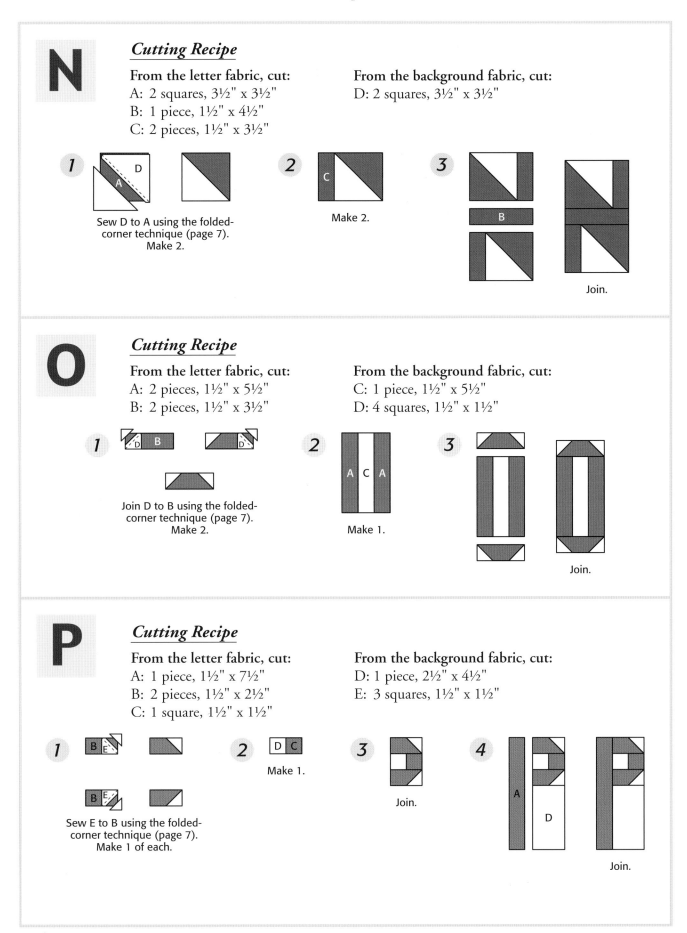

N

Cutting Recipe

From the letter fabric, cut:
A: 2 squares, 3½" x 3½"
B: 1 piece, 1½" x 4½"
C: 2 pieces, 1½" x 3½"

From the background fabric, cut:
D: 2 squares, 3½" x 3½"

1
Sew D to A using the folded-corner technique (page 7).
Make 2.

2
Make 2.

3
Join.

O

Cutting Recipe

From the letter fabric, cut:
A: 2 pieces, 1½" x 5½"
B: 2 pieces, 1½" x 3½"

From the background fabric, cut:
C: 1 piece, 1½" x 5½"
D: 4 squares, 1½" x 1½"

1
Join D to B using the folded-corner technique (page 7).
Make 2.

2
Make 1.

3
Join.

P

Cutting Recipe

From the letter fabric, cut:
A: 1 piece, 1½" x 7½"
B: 2 pieces, 1½" x 2½"
C: 1 square, 1½" x 1½"

From the background fabric, cut:
D: 1 piece, 2½" x 4½"
E: 3 squares, 1½" x 1½"

1
Sew E to B using the folded-corner technique (page 7).
Make 1 of each.

2
Make 1.

3
Join.

4
Join.

Cutting Recipe

From the letter fabric, cut:
A: 2 pieces, 1½" x 5½"
B: 2 pieces, 1½" x 3½"

From the background fabric, cut:
C: 1 piece, 1½" x 5½"
D: 4 squares, 1½" x 1½"

Piece *O* as shown on page 17.
Fuse a ½" x 1¾" strip of letter fabric
to the bottom-right corner.

Cutting Recipe

From the letter fabric, cut:
A: 1 piece, 1½" x 7½"
B: 1 piece, 1½" x 3½"
C: 3 pieces, 1½" x 2½"
D: 1 square, 1½" x 1½"

From the background fabric, cut:
E: 1 piece, 1½" x 3½"
F: 4 squares, 1½" x 1½"

1

Make 2.

Make 1.
Join F to C using the folded-
corner technique (page 7).

2
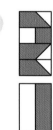
Make 1 of each.

3

Join.

4
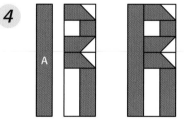
Join.

S

Cutting Recipe

From the letter fabric, cut:
A: 3 pieces, 1½" x 3½"
B: 1 piece, 1½" x 2½"
C: 4 squares, 1½" x 1½"

From the background fabric, cut:
D: 1 square, 2½" x 2½"
E: 1 piece, 1½" x 2½"
F: 8 squares, 1½" x 1½"

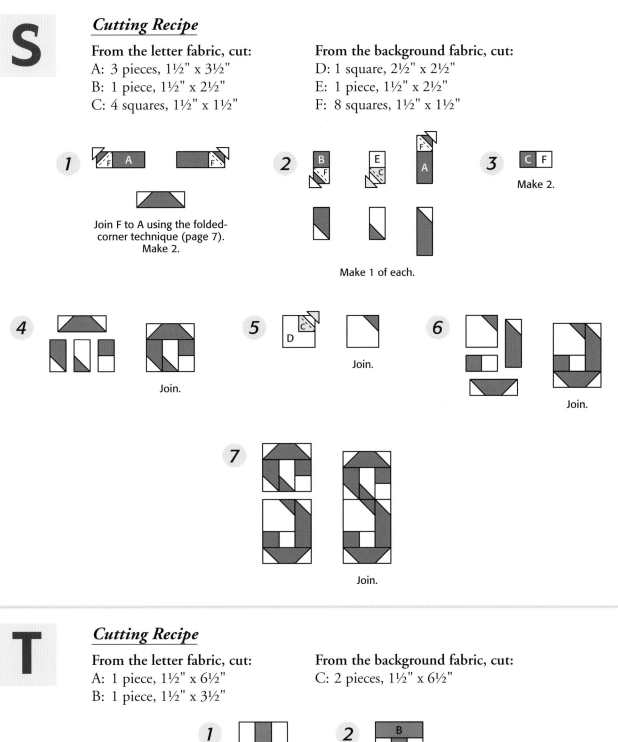

1 Join F to A using the folded-corner technique (page 7). Make 2.

2 Make 1 of each.

3 Make 2.

4 Join.

5 Join.

6 Join.

7 Join.

T

Cutting Recipe

From the letter fabric, cut:
A: 1 piece, 1½" x 6½"
B: 1 piece, 1½" x 3½"

From the background fabric, cut:
C: 2 pieces, 1½" x 6½"

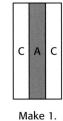

1 Make 1.

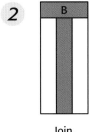

2 Join.

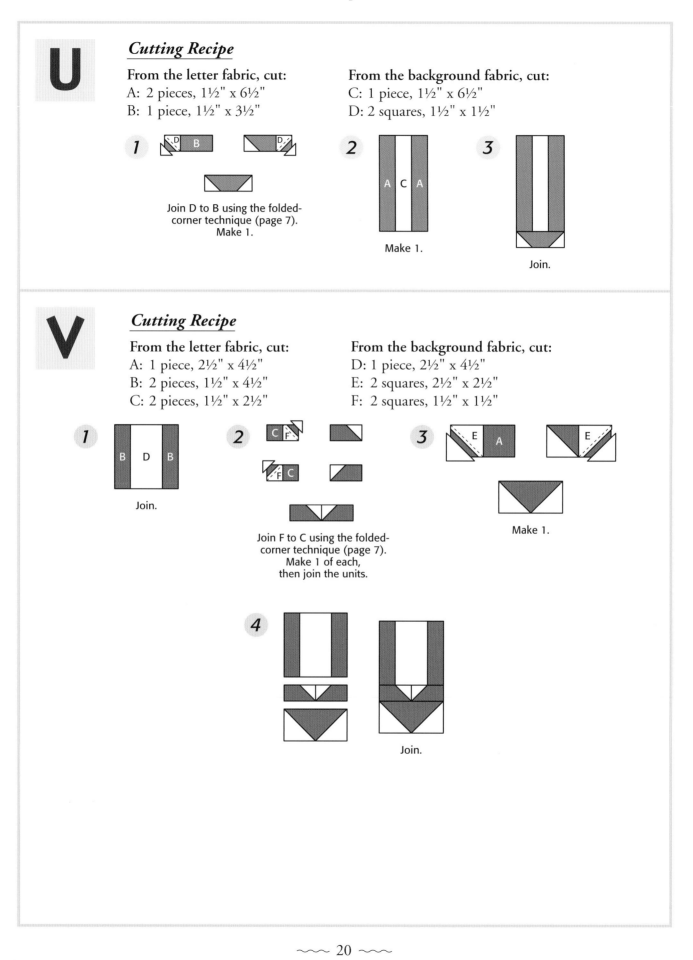

U

Cutting Recipe

From the letter fabric, cut:
A: 2 pieces, 1½" x 6½"
B: 1 piece, 1½" x 3½"

From the background fabric, cut:
C: 1 piece, 1½" x 6½"
D: 2 squares, 1½" x 1½"

1
Join D to B using the folded-corner technique (page 7).
Make 1.

2
A C A
Make 1.

3
Join.

V

Cutting Recipe

From the letter fabric, cut:
A: 1 piece, 2½" x 4½"
B: 2 pieces, 1½" x 4½"
C: 2 pieces, 1½" x 2½"

From the background fabric, cut:
D: 1 piece, 2½" x 4½"
E: 2 squares, 2½" x 2½"
F: 2 squares, 1½" x 1½"

1
B D B
Join.

2
C F
F C
Join F to C using the folded-corner technique (page 7).
Make 1 of each,
then join the units.

3
E A
E
Make 1.

4
Join.

W

Cutting Recipe

From the letter fabric, cut:
A: 2 pieces, 1½" x 7½"
B: 1 square, 2½" x 2½"
C: 2 squares, 1½" x 1½"

From the background fabric, cut:
D: 1 piece, 2½" x 4½"
E: 1 piece, 1½" x 2½"
F: 4 squares, 1½" x 1½"

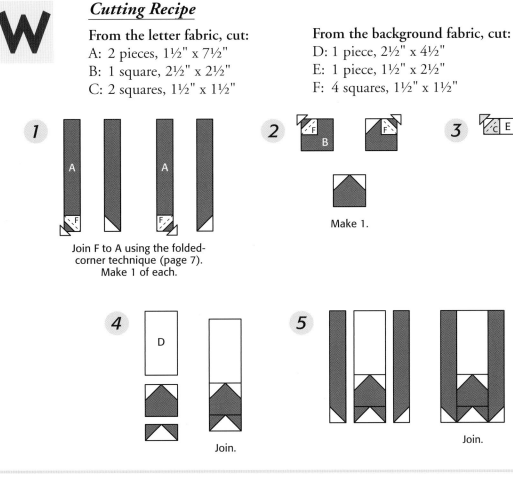

1

Join F to A using the folded-
corner technique (page 7).
Make 1 of each.

2

Make 1.

3

Make 1.

4

Join.

5

Join.

X

Cutting Recipe

From the letter fabric, cut:
A: 4 squares, 2½" x 2½"
B: 2 pieces, 1½" x 2½"
C: 2 squares, 1½" x 1½"

From the background fabric, cut:
D: 5 squares, 2½" x 2½"
E: 1 piece, 1½" x 2½"
F: 4 squares, 1½" x 1½"

1

Join D to A using the folded-
corner technique (page 7).
Make 4.

2

Join F to the letter-fabric corner
of each unit from step 1.

3

Join the units from step 2,
rotating them as shown.

4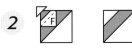

Make 1 of each.

5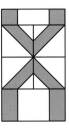

Join.

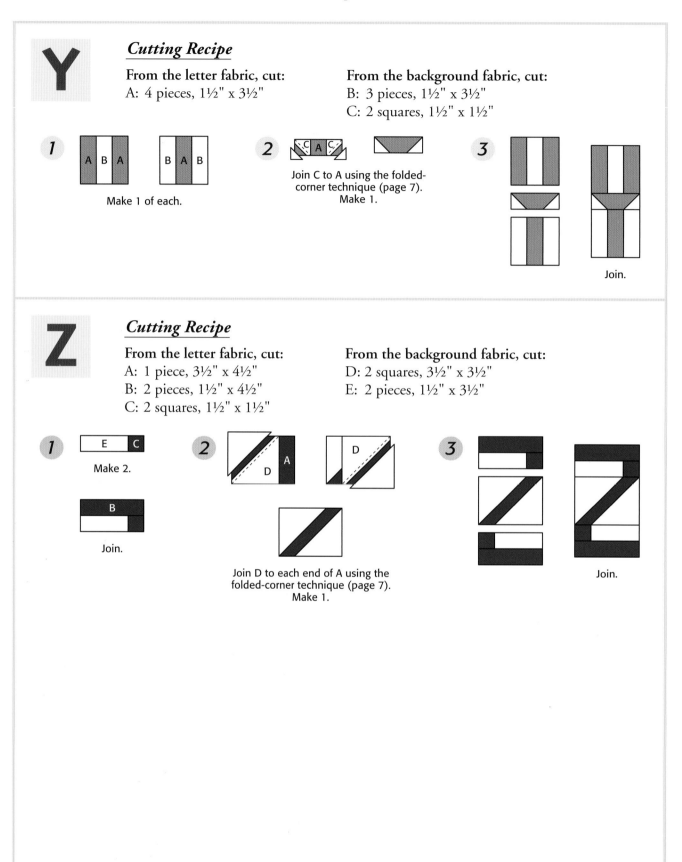

Y

Cutting Recipe

From the letter fabric, cut:
A: 4 pieces, 1½" x 3½"

From the background fabric, cut:
B: 3 pieces, 1½" x 3½"
C: 2 squares, 1½" x 1½"

1 A B A   B A B
Make 1 of each.

2 C A C
Join C to A using the folded-corner technique (page 7).
Make 1.

3 Join.

Z

Cutting Recipe

From the letter fabric, cut:
A: 1 piece, 3½" x 4½"
B: 2 pieces, 1½" x 4½"
C: 2 squares, 1½" x 1½"

From the background fabric, cut:
D: 2 squares, 3½" x 3½"
E: 2 pieces, 1½" x 3½"

1 E C
Make 2.

B
Join.

2 D A   D
Join D to each end of A using the folded-corner technique (page 7).
Make 1.

3 Join.

Baskets

Quilt Size: 35" x 29"

*The Basket block is one of my favorites. This block gives an antique
feel to any quilt. In this quilt, the pink-and-brown color combination takes us
back to days gone by—it looks like a quilt that Grandma would have made.*
~ Tammy

Materials

Yardage is based on 42"-wide fabric.

⅞ yard of brown solid for pieced letters, outer border, and binding*

⅜ yard of brown print for sashing strips

⅜ yard of pink check for letter backgrounds

¼ yard *each* of 4 assorted pinks for Basket blocks

¼ yard *each* of 4 assorted browns for Basket blocks

¼ yard of pink stripe for inner border

1 yard of backing fabric

35" x 41" piece of batting

Yardage is sufficient for single-fold binding. Buy ¼ yard extra for double-fold binding.

Cutting

Refer to "The Alphabet" on page 11 for cutting the pieces needed for the letters and letter backgrounds.

From the brown solid, cut:
✦ Pieces needed for the letters *(BASKETS)*
✦ 4 outer-border strips, 3" x 42"
✦ 4 strips, 1½" x 42" (for *single-fold* binding)

From the pink check, cut:
✦ Pieces needed for the letter backgrounds *(BASKETS)*
✦ 6 strips, 1½" x 7½"

From *each* of the assorted pinks, cut:
✦ 1 square, 4⅞" x 4⅞"; cut the squares in half once diagonally to yield 2 triangles (8 total)
✦ 1 square, 2⅞" x 2⅞"; cut the squares in half once diagonally to yield 2 triangles (8 total)
✦ 2 strips, 1½" x 6½" (8 total)
✦ 2 strips, 1½" x 5½" (8 total)
✦ 4 strips, 1½" x 3½" (16 total)

From *each* of the assorted browns, cut:
✦ 1 square, 4⅞" x 4⅞"; cut the squares in half once diagonally to yield 2 triangles (8 total)
✦ 2 squares, 1⅞" x 1⅞"; cut the squares in half once diagonally to yield 4 triangles (16 total)

From the brown print for sashing, cut:
✦ 5 strips, 1½" x 42"; crosscut into 4 strips, 1½" x 29½", and 10 strips, 1½" x 6½"

From the pink stripe, cut:
✦ 4 inner-border strips, 1" x 42"

Piecing the Letters

1. Piece the letter blocks needed for the word *BASKETS* referring to "The Alphabet" on page 11. Use the brown solid for the letters and the pink check for the letter backgrounds.

2. Sew the six 1½" x 7½" pink check strips between the letters as shown.

Constructing the Basket Blocks

You have enough pieces of each pink and brown fabric for two Basket blocks. Select one pink and one brown for each basket, but feel free to mix up your combinations so that no two blocks are exactly alike.

1. Stitch together a large pink triangle and a large brown triangle.

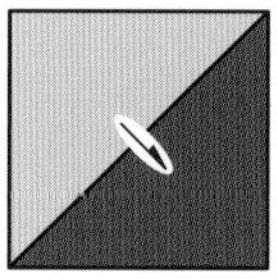

2. Stitch a small brown triangle to the end of a 3½" pink strip. Repeat to make two units, noting the position of the brown triangle in each unit.

Make 1 of each.

3. Stitch these units to the triangle square from step 1. Then add a small pink triangle to the corner as shown. Sew a 5½" pink strip to the left side of the block. Then add a 6½" pink strip to the top of the block.

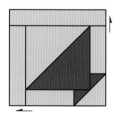

Basket block.
Make 8.

4. Using the basket-handle pattern below, prepare a matching brown handle for appliqué. We used fusible appliqué, and then blanket-stitched by machine around the edges of the handles. Refer to "Appliqué" on page 7 for more information.

5. Repeat steps 1–4 to make a total of eight Basket blocks.

Assembling the Quilt Top

1. Lay out the Basket blocks in two rows of four baskets each, paying careful attention to the orientation of each basket. Place the 6½" brown print strips between the blocks and at both ends of each row. When you are satisfied with the basket placement, stitch each row of blocks and sashing strips together. Press the seam allowances toward the sashing strips. Sew the 29½" brown print strips to the top and bottom of each basket row. Press the seam allowances toward the brown strips.

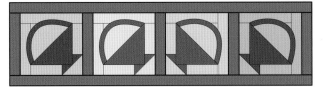

Make 2.

2. Stitch the basket rows to the top and bottom of the pieced letter row. Press the seam allowances toward the brown strips.

3. For the inner border, trim two of the pink stripe strips to 23½" long. Stitch these to the sides of the quilt. Press the seam allowances toward the border. Trim the remaining two pink stripe strips

to 30½" long and stitch them to the top and bottom of the quilt. Press the seam allowances toward the border.

4. For the outer border, trim two of the 3"-wide brown solid strips to 24½" long. Stitch them to the sides of the quilt and press the seam allowances toward the brown borders. Trim the remaining 3"-wide brown strips to 35½" long and stitch them to the top and bottom of the quilt. Press as before.

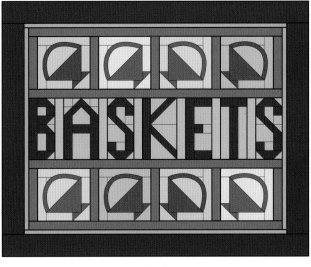

Quilt plan

Finishing

Layer the quilt top, batting, and backing. Baste the layers together and quilt as desired. In the quilt shown, the letters and baskets were outline quilted. Flowers were quilted in the background of the baskets and a chain of loops was quilted in the outer border. Bind the quilt using the 1½"-wide brown solid strips, referring to page 9 for more information.

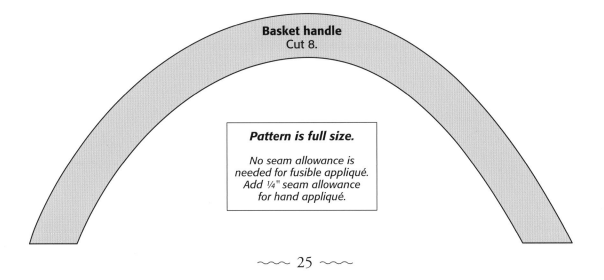

Basket handle
Cut 8.

Pattern is full size.

No seam allowance is needed for fusible appliqué. Add ¼" seam allowance for hand appliqué.

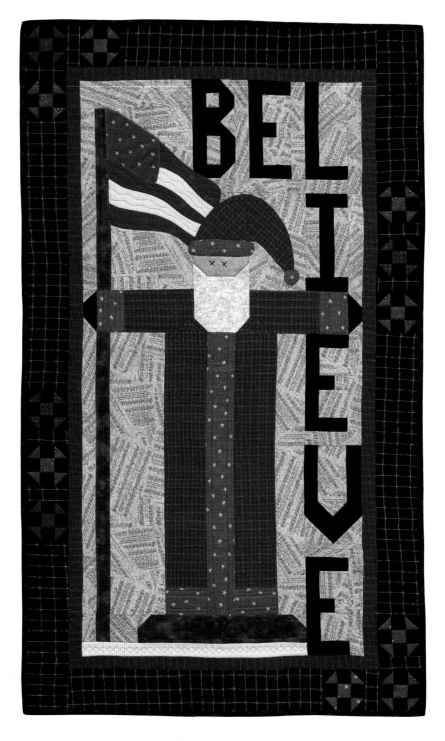

Believe

Quilt Size: 28" x 49"

Do you believe in Santa Claus? Seeing the excitement of a young child after he receives that special toy he has dreamed of is enough to make me believe. This Santa also believes in the United States, and he proudly waves the American flag.

~ Tammy

Materials

Yardage is based on 42"-wide fabric.
¾ yard of tan print for background
½ yard of black solid for pieced letters, Santa's mittens, and Shoo Fly blocks
½ yard of black plaid for pieced outer border
½ yard of red plaid for Santa's coat and hat
⅜ yard of red solid for flag
¼ yard of red print for Santa's coat trim, hat trim, and pom-pom
¼ yard of mottled black for Santa's boots and flagpole
¼ yard of cream stripe for flag and snow under Santa's feet
¼ yard of blue star print for star field on flag
¼ yard or scrap of cream print for Santa's beard
¼ yard of tan solid for Santa's face
¼ yard of red stripe for inner border
¼ yard *each* of 4 assorted reds for Shoo Fly blocks
¼ yard of black print for binding*
1¾ yards of backing fabric
34" x 55" piece of batting
Brown embroidery floss

Yardage is sufficient for single-fold binding. Buy ¼ yard extra for double-fold binding.

Cutting

Refer to "The Alphabet" on page 11 for cutting the pieces needed for the letters and letter backgrounds.

From the black solid, cut:
- Pieces needed for the letters *(BELIEVE)*
- 2 pieces, 1½" x 3½"
- 24 squares, 1⅞" x 1⅞"; cut the squares in half once diagonally to yield 48 triangles
- 48 squares, 1½" x 1½"

From the tan print, cut:
- Pieces needed for the letter backgrounds *(BELIEVE)*
- 2 strips, 1½" x 42"
- 1 piece, 6½" x 13½"
- 1 strip, 4½" x 42"; crosscut into:
  1 piece, 4½" x 20½"
  1 piece, 4½" x 7½"
  1 square, 4½" x 4½"
- 1 strip, 2½" x 42"; crosscut into:
  1 strip, 2½" x 20½"
  1 piece, 2½" x 8½"
  1 square, 2½" x 2½"

- 1 strip, 1½" x 42"; crosscut into:
  1 strip, 1½" x 20½"
  1 strip, 1½" x 13½"
  1 piece, 1½" x 2½"
  6 squares, 1½" x 1½"

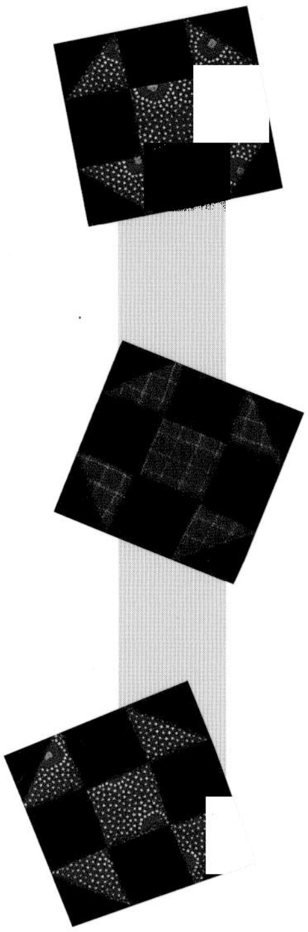

From the red print, cut:
- 1 strip, 2½" x 20½"
- 4 pieces, 2½" x 3½"

From the red plaid, cut:
- 2 strips, 3½" x 18½"
- 2 pieces, 3½" x 5½"
- 2 squares, 1½" x 1½"

From the cream print, cut:
- 1 square, 4½" x 4½"
- 2 squares, 1½" x 1½"

From the tan solid, cut:
- 1 piece, 2½" x 4½"

From the mottled black, cut:
- 2 pieces, 2½" x 6½"
- 1 strip, 1½" x 42"; crosscut into:
  1 strip, 1½" x 20½"
  1 strip, 1½" x 13½"
  1 piece, 1½" x 2½"

From the cream stripe, cut:
- 1 strip, 1½" x 16½"

From the assorted reds, cut:
- 24 squares, 1⅞" x 1⅞"; cut the squares in half once diagonally to yield 48 triangles
- 12 squares, 1½" x 1½"

From the red stripe, cut:
- 2 inner-border strips, 1½" x 41½"*
- 2 inner-border strips, 1½" x 22½"
If your fabric is not at least 41½" wide, you will need to cut an additional 1½"-wide strip and piece the inner-border strips to be long enough for your quilt.

From the black plaid, cut:
- 3 strips, 3½" x 42"; crosscut into:
  1 border strip, 3½" x 20½"
  1 border strip, 3½" x 19½"
  2 border strips, 3½" x 18½"
  1 border strip, 3½" x 12½"
  1 border strip, 3½" x 11½"
  8 border pieces, 3½" x 1½"

From the black print, cut:
- 5 strips, 1½" x 42" (for *single-fold* binding)

Piecing the Letters

1. Piece the letter blocks needed for the word *BELIEVE* referring to "The Alphabet" on page 11. Use the black solid for the letters and the tan print for the letter backgrounds.

2. From the two 1½" x 42" tan print strips, cut the following pieces to use as spacers between the letters:

   1 piece, 1½" x 12½"
   6 pieces, 1½" x 7½"
   2 pieces, 1½" x 4½"

3. Stitch the *B, E,* and *L* blocks together with three of the 7½" spacer strips as shown. Add the 12½" spacer strip to the bottom of this unit.

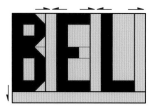

4. Sew a 7½" spacer strip to the right side of the *I* and both remaining *E* blocks. (There is no spacer on the *V* block.)

5. Stitch the *E, V,* and *E* blocks together vertically, sewing the two 4½" spacer strips between the blocks as shown. Set this unit aside.

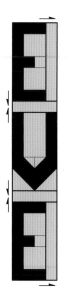

Constructing the Santa Unit

1. Join a 1½" tan print square to each end of a 1½" x 3½" black solid rectangle, using the folded-corner technique on page 7. Make two of these units for mittens.

Make 2.

2. To make the arms, sew each mitten from step 1 to a 2½" x 3½" red print piece. Then add a 3½" x 5½" red plaid piece as shown.

Make 2.

3. Stitch the 4½" x 7½" tan print rectangle to the left of the *I* block. Sew this unit to the top of one of the arm units as shown, making sure the pieces are oriented correctly.

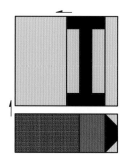

4. To make the face and beard, join the two 1½" cream print squares to the bottom corners of the 2½" x 4½" tan solid rectangle using the folded-corner technique. In the same manner, sew the two 1½" red plaid squares to two adjacent corners of the 4½" cream print square. Sew this unit to the bottom of the tan solid rectangle, and attach the 4½" tan print square to the top of this unit.

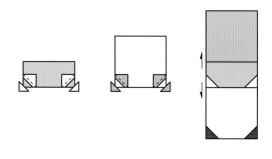

5. Stitch the unit from step 4 to the side of the unit from step 3. Then stitch the *BEL* unit to the top as shown.

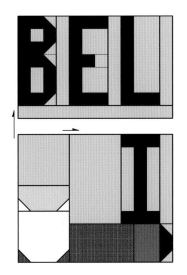

6. Stitch together the tan print and mottled black 1½" x 13½" strips. Join these to the 6½" x 13½" tan print strip. Sew the 2½" x 8½" tan print rectangle to the top of this unit and the remaining arm unit from step 2 to the bottom of the unit as shown.

7. Stitch the unit from step 6 to the left of the unit from step 5.

8. Sew a 2½" x 3½" red print piece to the bottom of a 3½" x 18½" red plaid strip. Repeat to make two of these units. Then stitch these units to either side of the 2½" x 20½" red print strip.

Sew the 2½" x 20½" tan print strip to the right side of this unit. To the left of this unit, sew the 4½" x 20½" tan print strip, the 1½" x 20½" mottled black strip, and the 1½" x 20½" tan print strip. This is the coat unit.

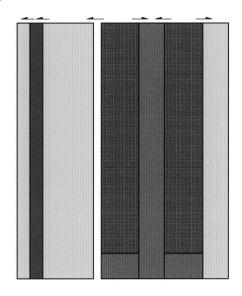

9. Join a 1½" tan print square to a 2½" x 6½" mottled black rectangle using the folded-corner technique. Repeat this process with the remaining tan print square and mottled black rectangle, noting the position of the squares.

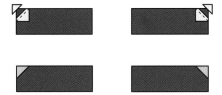

Make 1 of each.

10. Stitch the two units from step 9 together so that the tan triangles are in the outer corners. Stitch the tan print and mottled black 1½" x 2½" pieces together along the long edges. Sew the 2½" tan print square to this unit. Join the two units and sew the 1½" x 16½" cream stripe strip to the bottom of this boot unit.

11. Stitch the boot unit to the bottom of the coat unit. Then add the *EVE* unit to the right side. Stitch the two units together.

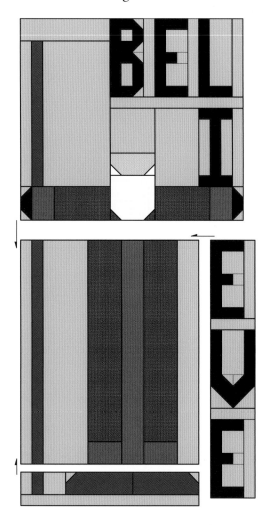

Appliqué

Using the appliqué patterns on pages 32–33, prepare the flag base, two stripes, and the star field using the red solid, cream stripe, and blue star print. Also prepare the stocking hat from red plaid and the hat trim and pom-pom from red print. We used fusible appliqué and then stitched around the appliqués with a machine blanket stitch. Refer to "Appliqué" on page 7 for more information.

1. Referring to the color photograph on page 26 for placement, appliqué the flag base first. Then add the two stripes followed by the star field.

2. Appliqué the hat onto Santa's head and then add the hat trim and pom-pom.

3. Stitch two large cross-stitches for Santa's eyes using three strands of brown embroidery floss.

Adding the Borders

1. Sew the 41½" red stripe inner-border strips to the sides of the quilt. Press the seam allowances toward the borders. Sew the 22½" inner-border strips to the top and bottom of the quilt. Press as before.

2. Construct 12 Shoo Fly blocks. For each block use four matching assorted red triangles, one assorted red square, four black solid triangles, and four black solid squares. Stitch the red and black triangles together to make triangle squares. Lay out the triangle squares and the plain squares as shown. Sew the units together in rows and then sew the rows together.

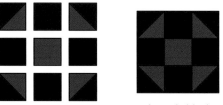

Shoo Fly block.
Make 12.

3. Sew a Shoo Fly block to one end of an 18½" black plaid strip. Sew a 1½" x 3½" black plaid piece to the opposite side of the Shoo Fly block. Repeat to make two of these units and sew them to the top and bottom of the quilt top. Press the seam allowances toward the plaid fabric.

4. Stitch the remaining Shoo Fly blocks together to create two units, separating each block with the 1½" x 3½" black plaid pieces as shown. You'll need two sets of three blocks and two sets of two blocks.

 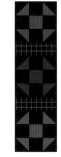

Make 2   Make 2

5. Assemble the left border in the following order: two-unit Shoo Fly, 19½" black plaid strip, three-unit Shoo Fly, 12½" black plaid strip. Press all seam allowances toward the black plaid pieces.

For the right border, sew the pieces in the following order: 11½" black plaid strip, three-unit Shoo Fly, 20½" black plaid strip, two-unit Shoo Fly. Press the seam allowances toward the black plaid pieces. Join the border strips to the quilt top and press the seam allowances toward the quilt center.

Finishing

Layer the quilt top, batting, and backing. Baste the layers together and quilt as desired. In the quilt shown, the background is stipple quilted. Straight lines were quilted to define the coat and flagpole. Wavy lines were quilted in the flag. The inner border was quilted with a continuous line of small hearts. The black plaid in the outer border was quilted with cross-hatching, and the Shoo Fly blocks were quilted in the ditch. Bind the quilt using the 1½" black print strips, referring to page 9 for more information.

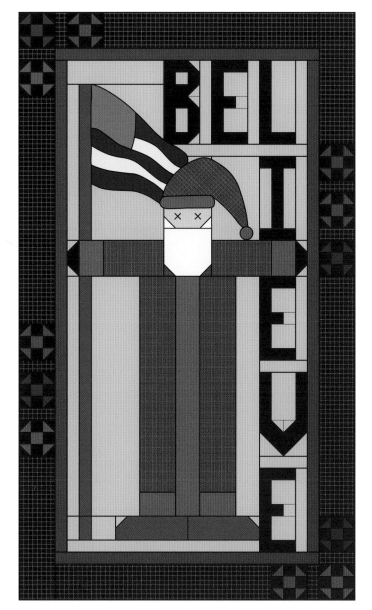

Quilt plan

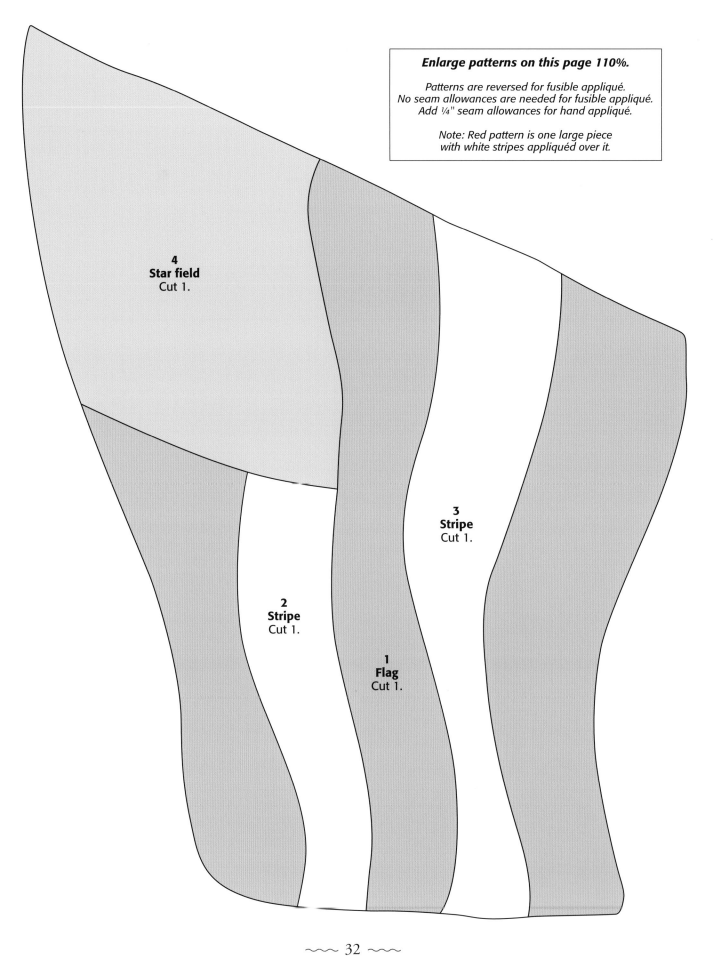

Enlarge patterns on this page 110%.

Patterns are reversed for fusible appliqué.
No seam allowances are needed for fusible appliqué.
Add ¼" seam allowances for hand appliqué.

Note: Red pattern is one large piece
with white stripes appliquéd over it.

4
Star field
Cut 1.

3
Stripe
Cut 1.

2
Stripe
Cut 1.

1
Flag
Cut 1.

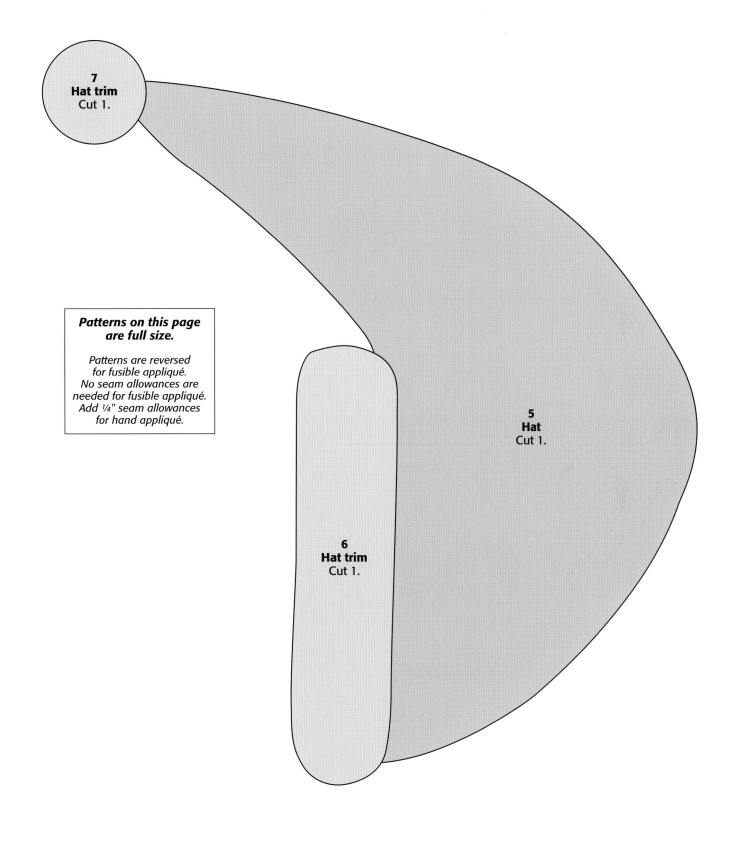

7
Hat trim
Cut 1.

***Patterns on this page
are full size.***

*Patterns are reversed
for fusible appliqué.
No seam allowances are
needed for fusible appliqué.
Add ¼" seam allowances
for hand appliqué.*

5
Hat
Cut 1.

6
Hat trim
Cut 1.

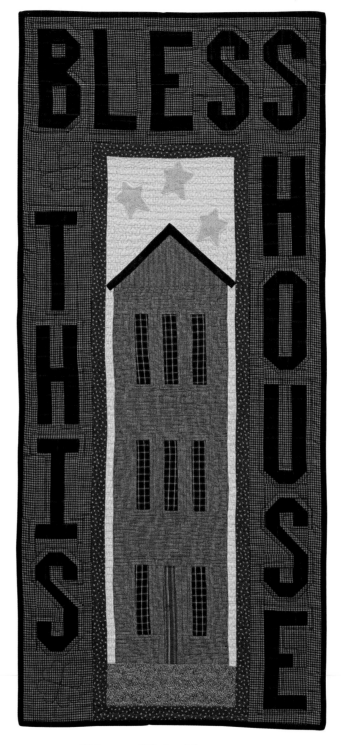

Bless This House

Quilt Size: 21" x 50"

Growing up in Iowa, I saw the simple sentiment "Bless This House" hanging on the wall in almost everyone's home—including mine. It was a quiet reminder to ask the Lord to bless our family and home and anyone who entered in.
- Tammy

Materials

Yardage is based on 42"-wide fabric.

¾ yard of black check for letter backgrounds

⅝ yard of black stripe for pieced letters and binding*

⅜ yard of gray for house

¼ yard of tan stripe for house background

¼ yard of black plaid for windows

¼ yard of green print for grass

¼ yard of red print for border around house

¼ yard of gold print for star appliqués

⅛ yard of black solid wool felt or cotton for roof appliqués

⅛ yard of red stripe for door

1⅝ yards of backing fabric

27" x 56" piece of batting

*Yardage is sufficient for single-fold binding. Buy ¼ yard extra for double-fold binding.

Cutting

Refer to "The Alphabet" on page 11 for cutting the pieces needed for the letters and letter backgrounds.

From the black stripe, cut:
- ◆ Pieces needed for the letters (*BLESS THIS HOUSE*)
- ◆ 4 strips, 1½" x 42" (for *single-fold* binding)

From the black check, cut:
- ◆ Pieces needed for the letter backgrounds (*BLESS THIS HOUSE*)
- ◆ 2 squares, 5½" x 5½"
- ◆ 2 strips, 1½" x 41½"*
- ◆ 2 strips, 1½" x 31½"
- ◆ 2 strips, 1½" x 21½"
- ◆ 6 pieces, 1½" x 7½"
- ◆ 9 pieces, 1½" x 3½"

*If your fabric is not 41½" wide after removing the selvages, you will need to piece strips together to achieve this length.

From the black plaid, cut:
- ◆ 8 pieces, 1½" x 5½"

From the gray, cut:
- ◆ 3 pieces, 4½" x 8½"
- ◆ 1 piece, 2½" x 8½"
- ◆ 2 pieces, 2½" x 4"
- ◆ 6 pieces, 2" x 5½"
- ◆ 6 pieces, 1½" x 5½"

From the red stripe, cut:
- ◆ 1 piece, 1½" x 7½"

From the tan, cut:
- ◆ 1 piece, 5½" x 9½"
- ◆ 2 squares, 4½" x 4½"
- ◆ 2 strips, 1" x 31½"

From the green print, cut:
- ◆ 1 piece, 3½" x 9½"

From the red print, cut:
- ◆ 2 inner-border strips, 1½" x 39½"
- ◆ 2 inner-border strips, 1½" x 11½"

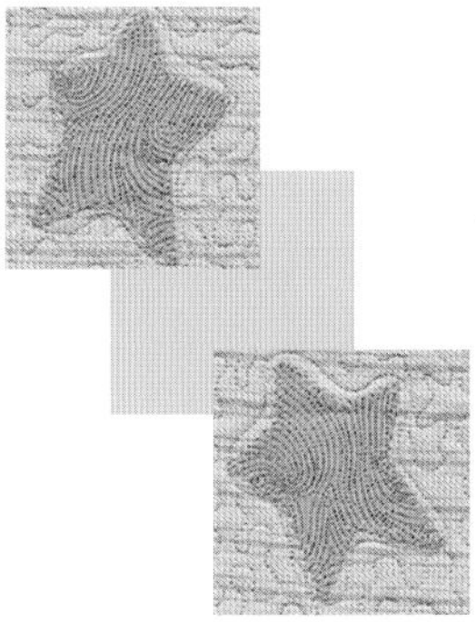

Piecing the Letters

1. Piece the letter blocks needed for the words *BLESS THIS HOUSE* referring to "The Alphabet." Use the black stripe for the letters and the black check for the letter backgrounds.

2. Stitch together the letter blocks to form the word *BLESS*, adding the six 1½" x 7½" black check spacer strips between the letters and at the beginning and end of the word unit. Then add the 1½" x 21½" black check strips to the top and bottom of the unit. Press all seam allowances toward the black check pieces.

3. Vertically join the letter blocks to form the word *THIS*, adding three 1½" x 3½" black check pieces between the letters. Sew the 1½" x 31½" black check strips to both sides of the word unit. Then stitch the 5½" black check squares to the top and bottom of this unit as shown. Press all seam allowances toward the black check pieces.

4. Stitch together the letter blocks to form the word *HOUSE* in the same manner, separating them with

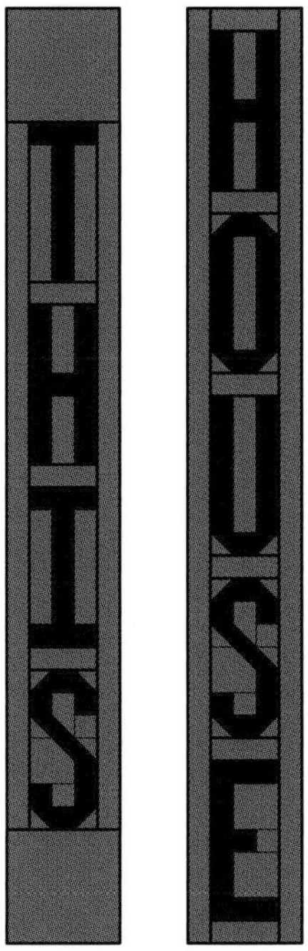

the 1½" x 3½" black check pieces, and sewing these pieces to the top and bottom of the unit also. Sew the 1½" x 41½" black check strips to the sides of the unit. Press toward the black check pieces. Set these units aside.

Constructing the House Block

1. To make the second- and third-floor window units, sew together three 1½" x 5½" black plaid pieces and two 1½" x 5½" gray pieces. Sew 2" x 5½" gray pieces to both sides of the unit. Make two units. Sew a 4½" x 8½" gray piece to the bottom of each. Stitch these two units together as shown, adding the 2½" x 8½" gray piece to the top of the unit.

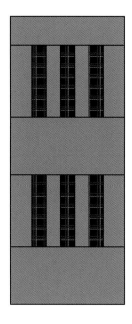

2. For the first floor, use the remaining 2" x 5½" gray pieces and the gray and black plaid 1½" x 5½" pieces. Arrange them as shown and stitch them together. Make one of each unit. Sew a 2½" x 4" gray piece to the bottom of each unit. Then join the units with the 1½" x 7½" red stripe door. Press all the seam allowances toward the gray pieces.

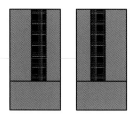

Make 1 of each.   Join.

3. Join the unit from step 2 to the bottom of the unit from step 1.

4. For the roof of the house, lay a 4½" tan square on top of the remaining 4½" x 8½" gray rectangle. Stitch diagonally and trim, referring to the folded-corner technique on page 7. Fold the resulting triangle over the seam and press. Repeat on the opposite corner of the rectangle.

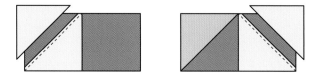

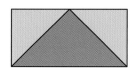

5. Add the roof unit to the top of the unit from step 3. Then add the 1" x 31½" tan strips to both sides of the house unit. Stitch the 5½" x 9½" tan piece to the top of the unit and the 3½" x 9½" green print piece to the bottom. Press each seam allowance toward the newly added piece.

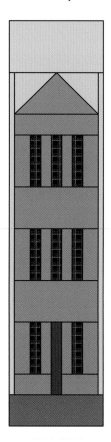

Assembling the Quilt Top

1. Sew the 39½" red print strips to the sides of the House block. Press the seam allowances toward the borders. Stitch the 11½" red borders to the top and bottom to complete the house unit. Press the seam allowances toward the borders.

2. To define the roofline, cut two strips, ½" x 6¼", from wool felt or from cotton prepared with fusible web. Appliqué the roof pieces over the diagonal seams at the top of the house using a machine blanket stitch.

3. Use the gold fabric and the star pattern below to appliqué three stars over the house. Refer to the quilt plan for placement. We used fusible appliqué and then added a machine blanket stitch around the edges of the appliqués. Refer to "Appliqué" on page 7 for more information.

4. Stitch the *THIS* word unit to the left side of the House block and stitch the *HOUSE* word unit to the right side. Then add the *BLESS* word unit to the top to complete the quilt top. Press all seam allowances toward the red inner border.

Finishing

Layer the quilt top, batting, and backing. Baste the layers together and quilt as desired. In the quilt shown, the letters were outlined with machine quilting. The house was quilted in a squarish stipple pattern to resemble bricks and the background of the house was meander quilted. The red border was quilted with a single wavy line. Bind the quilt using the 1½" black stripe strips, referring to page 9 for more information.

Quilt plan

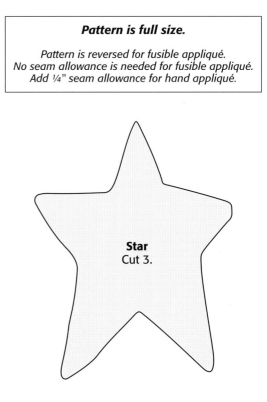

Pattern is full size.

Pattern is reversed for fusible appliqué.
No seam allowance is needed for fusible appliqué.
Add ¼" seam allowance for hand appliqué.

Star
Cut 3.

Fresh Flowers

Quilt Size: 53" x 32"

*This quilt makes me smile. I love flowers and can never have enough of them.
(The same goes for fabric.) The wagon is overflowing with beautiful blooms
of every color that will brighten up any room of your house.
What a wonderful quilt to welcome spring!*
~Avis

Materials

Yardage is based on 42"-wide fabric.

1¾ yards of blue stripe for wagon background

1⅛ yards of light blue check for letter backgrounds

¾ yard of slate blue for letters

½ yard of green print for stems and leaves

¼ yard of brown print for wagon

¼ yard of mottled black for wagon wheels and handle

¼ yard of gray plaid for wagon tongue and
    wheel spokes

¼ yard *total* of assorted scraps in the following
    colors: 6 pinks, 3 purples, 3 reds, and 3 yellows

⅛ yard of yellowish green for flower centers

¼ yard of blue print for binding*

1⅞ yards of backing fabric

38" x 59" piece of batting

*Yardage is sufficient for single-fold binding. Buy ⅛ yard extra for double-fold binding.

Cutting

Refer to "The Alphabet" on page 11 for cutting the pieces needed for the letters and letter backgrounds.

From the blue stripe, cut on the *lengthwise* grain:
◆ 1 strip, 17½" x 53½"

From the slate blue, cut:
◆ Pieces needed for the letters *(FRESH FLOWERS and PER BUNCH)*
◆ 3 pieces, 1½" x 3½"
◆ 3 pieces, 1½" x 2½"
◆ 6 squares, 1½" x 1½"
◆ 1 piece, 1½" x 4½"

From the light blue check, cut on the *lengthwise* grain:
◆ 4 strips, 1½" x 53½"

From the remaining light blue check, cut:
◆ Pieces needed for the letter backgrounds *(FRESH FLOWERS and PER BUNCH)*
◆ 4 pieces, 4½" x 7½"
◆ 1 piece, 3½" x 7½"
◆ 19 pieces, 1½" x 7½"
◆ 1 piece, 1½" x 3½"
◆ 1 piece, 1½" x 2½"
◆ 11 squares, 1½" x 1½"
◆ 2 squares, 2½" x 2½"

From the blue print, cut:
◆ 5 strips, 1½" x 42" (for *single-fold* binding)

Appliqué

The appliqué patterns for this project are on pages 42 and 43. There is no pattern for the wagon; cut a rectangle 6" x 27" from the brown print prepared with fusible web for this piece. (If you prefer to hand appliqué, add seam allowances to the measurements given.)

We used fusible appliqué for everything except the stems, and machine blanket-stitched around each shape to add a decorative touch. You may use hand appliqué if you prefer. Prepare all the shapes first so that you can work on the placement arrangement before anything is fused or stitched in place.

1. Place the wagon and wagon wheels on the 17½" x 53½" blue stripe piece. In the quilt shown, the wagon is placed 8" from the top edge of the background fabric and 3" from the bottom. It is also slightly off-center from side to side—approximately 12½" from the left edge and 14½" from the right edge. *Do not* fuse the shapes in place yet. Mark around the shapes with a chalk wheel or pencil so that you will know where to position the flowers, stems, and leaves.

2. Use the green print to make ½"-wide bias vines referring to "Making Bias Vines" on page 9. You'll need approximately 60" of vines.

3. There are seven groups of flowers in the wagon. Cut the bias vines in the following lengths, which include ¼" extra on each end for tucking under the wagon and flowers. Referring to the photograph for placement, place them in order from left to right:

Group 1: 3¼", 4¼", and 2¾"
Group 2: 2", 4¼", and 1¾"
Group 3: 1½" (this stem is tucked under the main stem) and 4¾"
Group 4: 2½", 4½", and 2"

Group 5: 4¾" and 2½" (this stem is tucked under the main stem)
Group 6: 2", 4½", and 1¾"
Group 7: 4", 3", and 2¾"

Placement can be tricky so adjust the stems as necessary, making sure that they all fit into the wagon. When you are satisfied with the arrangement, appliqué the vines in place.

4. From the gray plaid, prepare a ¾" x 8½" strip for the wagon tongue appliqué. Place the end that joins the wagon 1½" from the bottom edge of the wagon. Lay the handle on top for placement purposes and adjust as necessary. When the tongue and handle placement is to your liking, appliqué both pieces.

5. Appliqué the wagon, followed by the wagon wheels, spokes, and wheel centers. Add the leaves and flowers.

Piecing the Letters

1. Piece the letter blocks needed for the words *FRESH FLOWERS* and *PER BUNCH* referring to "The Alphabet" on page 11. Use the slate blue for the letters and the light blue check for the letter backgrounds.

2. To make the *5¢* unit, lay a 1½" slate blue square on top of a 2½" check square. Stitch diagonally across the small square. Trim the corner triangle and turn the resulting triangle over the seam and press. Refer to "Folded Corners" on page 7 as needed. Repeat to make two of these units.

Make 2.

3. To one of the units from step 2, add a 1½" x 2½" slate blue piece to the top and a 1½" x 3½" slate blue piece to the left side. Press both seam allowances toward the slate blue pieces.

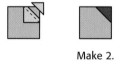

Make 1.

4. Join a 1½" slate blue square to a 1½" check square. Sew this unit to the top of a 1½" x 2½" slate blue piece as shown. Sew this unit to the bottom of the remaining unit from step 2.

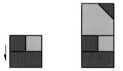

5. Using the folded-corner technique, sew 1½" check squares to each end of the 1½" x 4½" slate blue piece, noting the stitching angles. Sew this unit to the right side of the step 4 unit.

6. Join the two units to complete the number 5 unit.

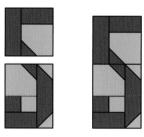

7. For the cent sign, stitch two 1½" check squares to opposite sides of a 1½" slate blue square. Make two. Also join a pair of 1½" check and slate blue squares, and a pair of 1½" x 2½" check and slate blue rectangles as shown.

Make 2.   Make 1 of each.

8. Using the folded-corner technique, sew a 1½" check square to one end of a 1½" x 3½" slate blue piece. Make two of these units. Then to one of them, sew another check square to the opposite end, changing the direction of the diagonal.

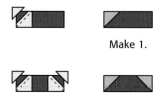

Make 1.

Make 1.

9. Stitch the units from steps 7 and 8 together as shown. Add the 1½" x 3½" check piece to the top of the unit to complete the cent sign.

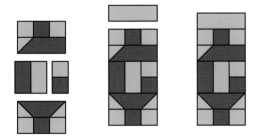

Assembling the Quilt Top

1. Assemble the top row of the quilt by sewing the letter blocks for *FRESH FLOWERS* together side by side, separated by the 1½" x 7½" check strips. Between the two words, use a 4½" x 7½" check piece instead of a 1½" strip. Press all seam allowances toward the check strips. To complete the row, sew a 1½" x 53½" strip to the top and bottom of the unit.

2. To make the bottom row of the quilt, sew the character blocks for *5¢ PER BUNCH* together side by side, separating the letters or symbols in each section with a 1½" x 7½" check strip. Then join the sections, separating them with the 4½" x 7½" check pieces. Add another of these

4½" x 7½" pieces to the right end of the row, and sew a 3½" x 7½" check piece to the left end of the row. To complete the row, sew a 1½" x 53½" strip to the top and bottom of the unit. Press as before.

3. Join the letter rows to the top and bottom of the appliqué section. Press the seam allowances toward the appliqué.

Finishing

Layer the quilt top, batting, and backing. Baste the layers together and quilt as desired. In the quilt shown, the letters and appliqué shapes were outline quilted by machine. The background was meander quilted, and the wagon was quilted with a series of parallel lines to give it the look of wood slats. Bind the quilt using the 1½" blue print strips, referring to page 9 for more information.

Quilt plan

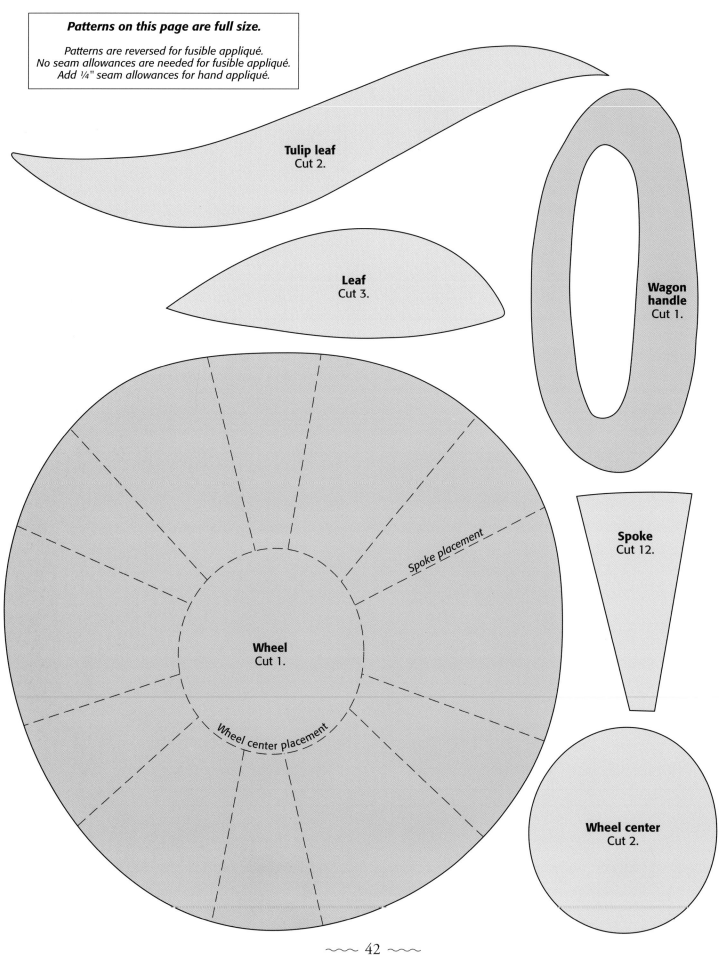

Patterns on this page are full size.

Patterns are reversed for fusible appliqué.
No seam allowances are needed for fusible appliqué.
Add ¼" seam allowances for hand appliqué.

Tulip leaf
Cut 2.

Leaf
Cut 3.

Wagon handle
Cut 1.

Wheel
Cut 1.

Spoke placement

Wheel center placement

Spoke
Cut 12.

Wheel center
Cut 2.

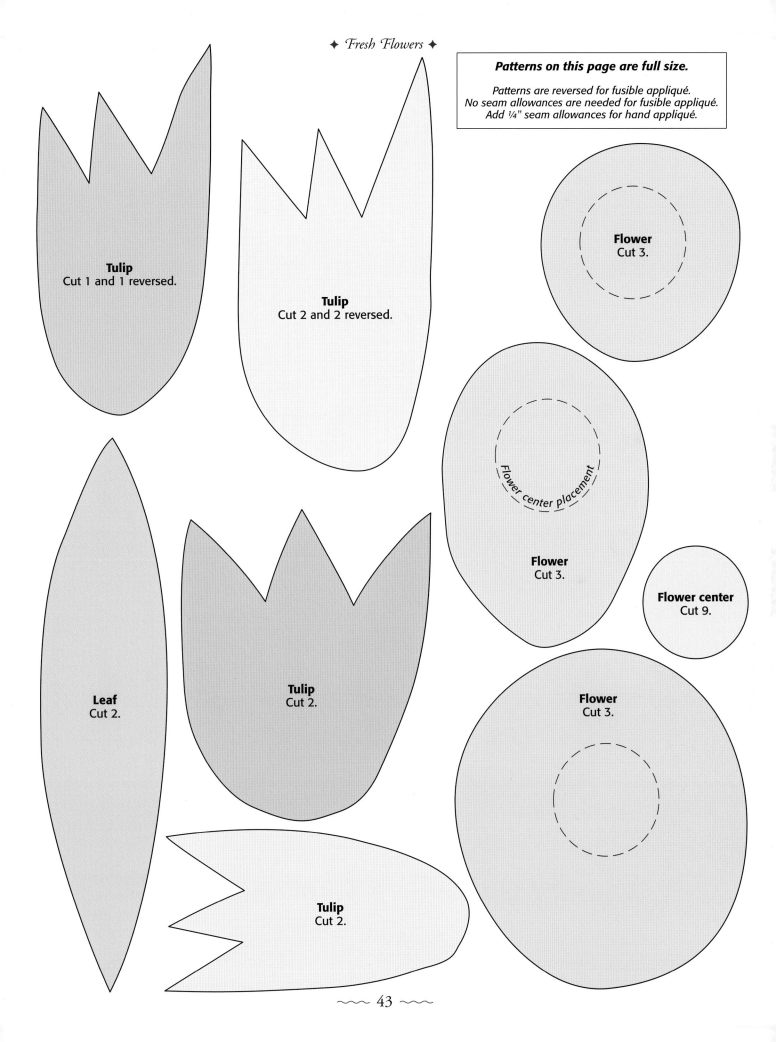

◆ *Fresh Flowers* ◆

Patterns on this page are full size.

*Patterns are reversed for fusible appliqué.
No seam allowances are needed for fusible appliqué.
Add ¼" seam allowances for hand appliqué.*

Tulip
Cut 1 and 1 reversed.

Tulip
Cut 2 and 2 reversed.

Flower
Cut 3.

Flower center placement

Flower
Cut 3.

Flower center
Cut 9.

Leaf
Cut 2.

Tulip
Cut 2.

Flower
Cut 3.

Tulip
Cut 2.

Old Glory

Quilt Size: 27" x 47"

*I collect baskets of every size, shape, and color. This wall hanging depicts
a favorite of mine—a tall, shapely basket holding our beloved flag.*
~Avis

Materials

Yardage is based on 42"-wide fabric.

1⅞ yards of tan print for background
1½ yards of navy stripe for outer border*
½ yard of brown print for basket
¼ yard of red print for stars
¼ yard of navy print for letters
¼ yard of navy for binding**
1⅝ yards of backing fabric
33" x 53" piece of batting
9" x 12" American flag on wooden dowel

*Yardage is for cutting the stripe lengthwise. If you prefer to piece the side borders, ¾ yard is sufficient.

**Yardage is sufficient for single-fold binding. Buy ⅜ yard for double-fold binding.

Cutting

Refer to "The Alphabet" on page 11 for cutting the pieces needed for the letters and letter backgrounds.

From the navy print, cut:
✦ Pieces needed for the letters (*OLD GLORY*)

From the tan print, cut:
✦ Pieces needed for the letter backgrounds (*OLD GLORY*)
✦ 1 strip, 11½" x 41½"*
✦ 1 strip, 2½" x 33½"
✦ 2 strips, 1½" x 23½"
✦ 1 strip, 5½" x 42"; crosscut into:
  1 piece, 5½" x 6½"
  1 piece, 5½" x 12½"
✦ 1 strip, 1½" x 42"; crosscut into:
  7 pieces, 1½" x 3½"
  1 piece, 1½" x 4½"
  1 piece, 1½" x 8½"

*If your fabric isn't at least 41½" wide, you'll need to cut this piece on the lengthwise grain.

From the navy stripe, cut on the *lengthwise* grain:
✦ 2 border strips, 3½" x 47½"

From the remaining navy stripe, cut:
✦ 2 border strips, 3½" x 21½"

From the navy for binding, cut:
✦ 4 strips, 1½" x 42" (for *single-fold* binding)

Piecing the Letters

1. Piece the letter blocks needed for the words *OLD GLORY* referring to "The Alphabet" on page 11. Use the navy print for the letters and the tan print for the letter backgrounds.

2. Assemble the *O, L,* and *D* blocks into a vertical strip, separating the letters with 1½" x 3½" tan pieces. Sew a 23½" tan strip to each side of the letters, and then sew the 5½" x 6½" tan piece to the top of the *O* block and the 5½" x 12½" tan piece to the bottom of the *D* block. Press the seam allowances toward the tan fabric.

3. Assemble the *L, O, R,* and *Y* blocks into a vertical strip, separating the letters with 1½" x 3½" tan strips. Sew these short tan strips to the top and bottom of the unit, too. Sew the 2½" x 33½" tan strip to the right side of the unit. Before attaching the *G* block to the top of the letter strip, sew the 1½" x 4½" tan strip to the top of the *G* block and attach the 1½" x 8½" tan strip to the right side of the *G* block. Then sew this unit to the top of the other letters.

Appliqué

We used fusible appliqué for most of the pieces and then stitched around the appliqués with a machine blanket stitch and matching thread. However, fusible appliqué doesn't work for the basket and rim because part of the basket needs to be loose from the background for the flagpole to be inserted after the quilt is finished. Refer to "Appliqué" on page 7 for more information.

1. Using the appliqué patterns on pages 47 and 48, prepare the three red stars for fusible appliqué. Appliqué the stars, referring to the quilt photograph for placement.

2. Prepare the basket handle for fusible appliqué. You'll need to enlarge the pattern pieces first. Appliqué the brown print basket handle in place.

3. Prepare the basket pattern by enlarging it and then tracing it onto freezer paper. Appliqué the basket in place by hand. Leave a 1" opening at the center of the top edge of the basket for the flag to be inserted.

4. Cut two pieces from the brown print using the basket rim pattern. Using your sewing machine, stitch the two pieces right sides together, sewing all the way around on the stitching line. Trim close to the stitching line. On one of the basket rim pieces, cut a small slit about 2" from one end. Turn the basket rim piece right side out and press well. With the slit facing the background piece, appliqué the rim on top of the basket. Leave a 1" segment open along both the top and bottom center of the rim, making sure the open area aligns with the open area of the basket itself.

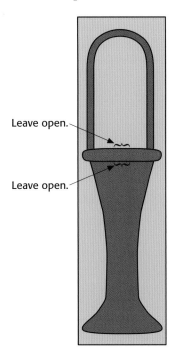

Leave open.

Leave open.

Assembling the Quilt Top

1. Sew the *OLD* word unit to the left side of the 11½" x 41½" tan rectangle and the *GLORY* word unit to the right side to complete the quilt center.

2. Sew the 3½" x 21½" navy stripe borders to the top and bottom of the quilt. Press the seam allowances toward the borders.

3. Sew the 3½" x 47½" navy stripe borders to both sides of the quilt. Press the seam allowances toward the borders.

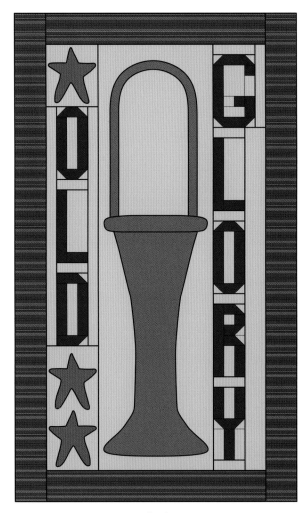

Quilt plan

Finishing

Layer the quilt top, batting, and backing. Baste the layers together and quilt as desired. Note: Do not quilt in the area where the flag will be inserted. If this area is sewn closed, you won't be able to insert the flag into the basket. In the quilt shown, the background was meander quilted. In the basket, we quilted two parallel vertical lines spaced about 1" apart to make a channel for the flagpole. The rest of the basket was quilted with a loop-the-loop motif. Straight lines were quilted in the border. Bind the quilt using the 1½" navy strips, referring to page 9 for more information. Add an American flag to complete the project.

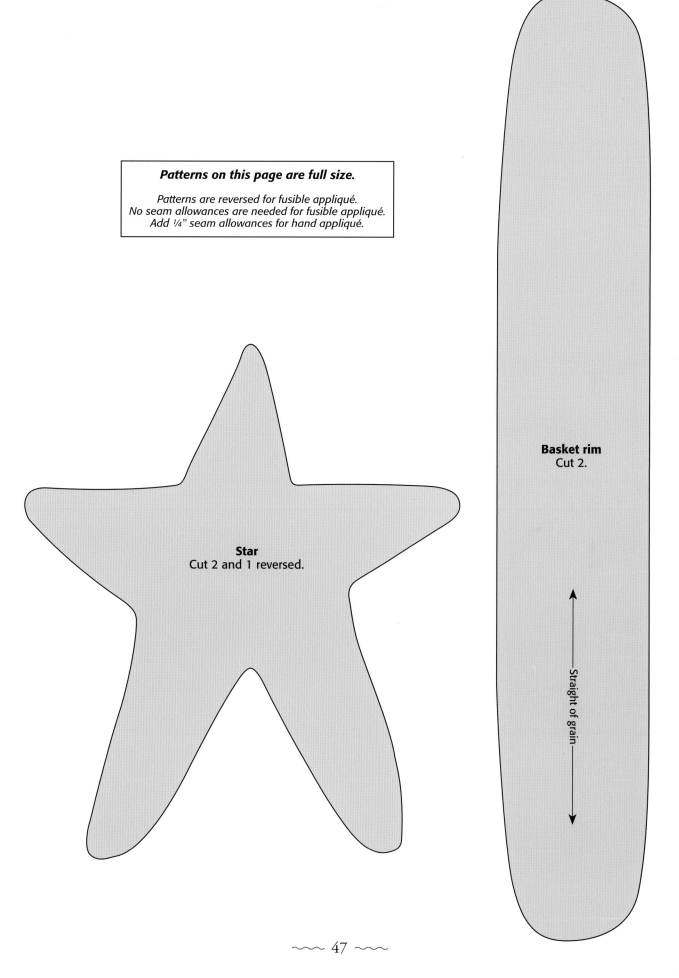

Patterns on this page are full size.

Patterns are reversed for fusible appliqué.
No seam allowances are needed for fusible appliqué.
Add ¼" seam allowances for hand appliqué.

Star
Cut 2 and 1 reversed.

Basket rim
Cut 2.

Straight of grain

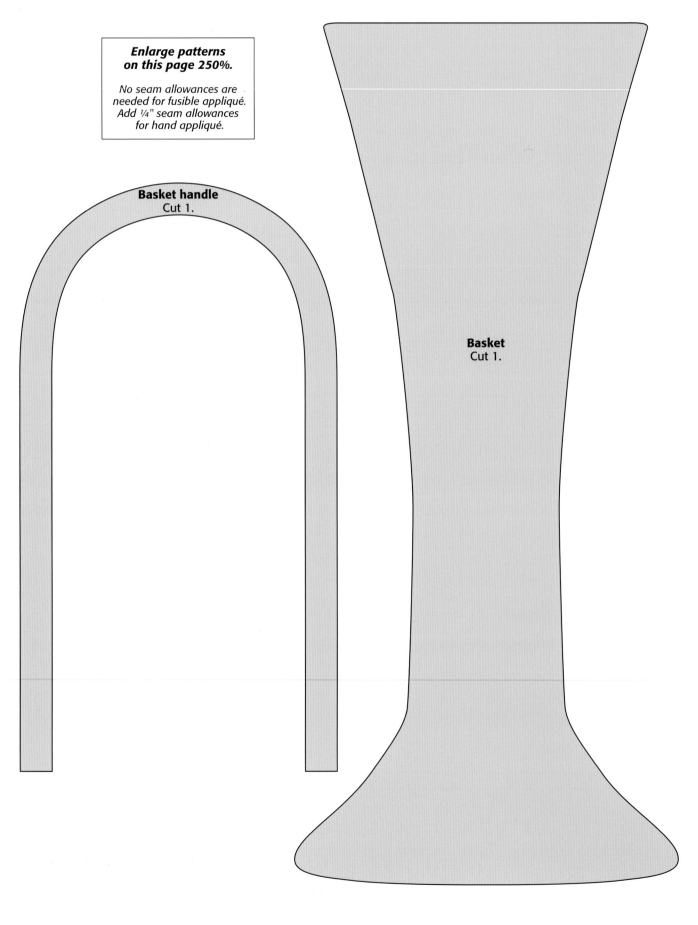

Enlarge patterns on this page 250%.

No seam allowances are needed for fusible appliqué. Add ¼" seam allowances for hand appliqué.

Basket handle
Cut 1.

Basket
Cut 1.

Peace and Plenty

Quilt Size: 30" x 55"

Pears are becoming one of my favorite folk-art objects. I love the stuffed wool pears that you find in gift shops. Toss a few of them in a bowl and you have a wonderful centerpiece. For this project, we pieced some pears and appliquéd others and the result is a striking wall quilt.

~ Tammy

Materials

Yardage is based on 42"-wide fabric.

¾ yard of brown print for outer border and binding*

½ yard of light brown print (background #1) for letter backgrounds, pear backgrounds, and spacers

⅜ yard of red plaid for inner border

⅜ yard of black stripe for letters

¼ yard *each* of 4 assorted beiges and light browns (backgrounds #2, #3, #4, and #5) for letter backgrounds, pear backgrounds, and spacers

¼ yard of brown check for bowl appliqué

¼ yard *each* of 5 light yellowish greens for pears

¼ yard *each* of 8 assorted dark fabrics for flying geese

⅛ yard *each* of 5 assorted beiges and light browns for flying geese

⅛ yard of medium yellowish green for leaf appliqués

Scrap or ⅛ yard of brown stripe for bowl rim

2" x 4" piece of brown wool for stem appliqués

2 yards of backing fabric

36" x 61" piece of batting

*Yardage is sufficient for single-fold binding. Buy ⅛ yard extra for double-fold binding.

Cutting

Refer to "The Alphabet" on page 11 for cutting the pieces needed for the letters and letter backgrounds.

From the black stripe, cut:
✦ Pieces needed for the letters *(P, E, A, E* and *L, E, N, T, Y.* Note: Only one *P* block is needed and the *C* block is pieced differently from the one in "The Alphabet"; see cutting below.)
✦ For the *C* block, cut:
    A: 1 piece, 1½" x 5½"
    B: 2 pieces, 1½" x 4½"
    C: 2 squares, 1½" x 1½"

From background #1, cut:
✦ Background pieces needed for the letters *(P, E, A, E,* and *Y)*
✦ For the *C* block background, cut:
    D: 1 square, 3½" x 3½"
    E: 2 pieces, 1½" x 2½"
    F: 4 squares, 1½" x 1½"
✦ 2 strips, 1½" x 23½"
✦ 6 strips, 1½" x 7½"
✦ 2 pieces, 4½" x 8½"
✦ 18 squares, 1½" x 1½"
✦ 7 pieces, 1½" x 3½"

From background #2, cut:
✦ Background pieces needed for the letter *L*
✦ 1 piece, 4½" x 7½"
✦ 1 piece, 3½" x 8½"

From background #3, cut:
✦ Background pieces needed for the letter *E*
✦ 1 piece, 8½" x 13½"
✦ 1 piece, 3½" x 16½"
✦ 1 piece, 1½" x 3½"

From background #4, cut:
✦ Background pieces needed for the letter *N*
✦ 1 piece, 5½" x 8½"
✦ 2 pieces, 1½" x 8½"
✦ 1 piece, 1½" x 4½"
✦ 2 pieces, 1½" x 3½"
✦ 6 squares, 1½" x 1½"

From background #5, cut:
✦ Background pieces needed for the letter *T*
✦ 1 piece, 3½" x 8½"
✦ 1 piece, 1½" x 8½"
✦ 3 pieces, 1½" x 3½"
✦ 6 squares, 1½" x 1½"

From *each* of the assorted yellowish greens for pears, cut:
✦ 1 piece, 4½" x 5½" (5 total)
✦ 1 piece, 2½" x 3½" (5 total)

From the assorted dark fabrics for flying geese, cut:
✦ 32 pieces, 2½" x 4½"

From the assorted beige and light brown fabrics for flying geese, cut:
✦ 64 squares, 2½" x 2½"

From the red plaid, cut:
✦ 2 inner-border strips, 1½" x 23½"
✦ 3 inner-border strips, 1½" x 42"

From the brown print, cut:
✦ 2 outer-border strips, 3" x 25½"
✦ 3 outer-border strips, 3" x 42"
✦ 5 binding strips, 1½" x 42" (for *single-fold* binding)

Piecing the Letters

1. Piece the letter blocks needed for the words *PEACE* and *PLENTY* referring to "The Alphabet" on page 11. Use the black stripe for the letters and the beiges and light browns for the letter backgrounds. Background #1 is used for the *P, E, A, C, E,* and *Y* blocks. Background #2 is used for the *L,* background #3 is used for the *E,* background #4 is used for the *N,* and background #5 is used for the *T* block.

   Note: In this quilt, the *C* block is made differently from the directions given in "The Alphabet." Make the *C* block as shown below.

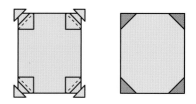

Join F to B using the folded-corner technique (page 7).
Make 2.

Sew C to E.
Make 2.
Join to the top
and bottom of D.

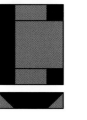

Sew A to the left
of the unit.

Join the units.

2. To construct the *PEACE* unit, sew the letters together, separating them with the 1½" x 7½" background #1 strips. Add background #1 strips to the beginning and end of the unit also. Press the seam allowances toward the spacer strips. Sew a 1½" x 23½" background #1 strip to the top and bottom of this unit. Press the seam allowances toward the strips. This is row 1 of the quilt.

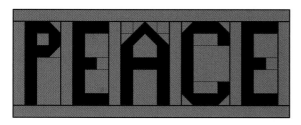

Row 1

Piecing the Pear Blocks

Construct five Pear blocks using one set of matching yellowish green pieces for each. Also make sure to use matching background pieces in each block. Three of the pears use background #1. The others use backgrounds #4 and #5. To make a Pear block:

1. Lay a 1½" background square on top of a 4½" x 5½" yellowish green rectangle. Using the folded-corner technique (page 7), stitch diagonally across the square as shown. Trim as indicated and turn the resulting triangle over the seam and press. Repeat this process on all four corners.

2. In the same manner, stitch a 1½" background square to the upper-left and upper-right corners of a yellowish green 2½" x 3½" piece. Stitch diagonally, trim, and press as shown. Add 1½" x 3½" background strips to each side of this unit.

3. Stitch the units from steps 1 and 2 together to complete a Pear block. Repeat to make all five blocks. Set aside.

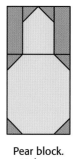

Pear block.
Make 5.

Piecing the Flying Geese

1. Lay a 2½" beige or light brown square on one corner of a 2½" x 4½" dark rectangle. Using the folded-corner technique, stitch, trim, and press. Repeat with a matching 2½" beige or light brown

square on the opposite end of the dark rectangle. Repeat to make a total of 32 flying-geese units.

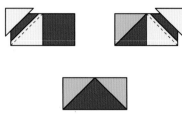

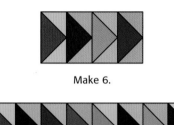

Make 32.

2. Stitch the flying-geese units together so that they are all pointing in the same direction as shown. Make six strips with four flying geese each, and one strip with eight flying geese.

Make 6.

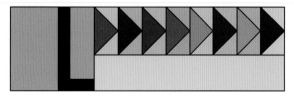

Make 1.

Assembling the Quilt Top

Throughout the quilt-top assembly, press the seam allowances toward the background pieces whenever possible.

1. Stitch the 4½" x 7½" background #2 piece to the left of the *L* block. Sew the 3½" x 16½" background #3 piece to the bottom of the eight-piece flying-geese unit with the flying geese pointing toward the right. Sew this unit to the right of the *L* block. Press. This is row 2 of the quilt.

Row 2

2. For row 3, stitch the 1½" x 3½" background #3 piece to the top of the *E* block. Then sew the 3½" x 8½" background #2 piece to the left of the *E* and the 8½" x 13½" background #3 piece to

the right of the *E* block. Finally, sew a four-unit flying-geese strip to the left of this unit (with the flying geese pointing upward).

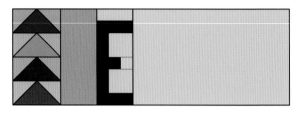

Row 3

3. For row 4, stitch the 1½" x 4½" background #4 piece to the top of the *N* block. Sew the 5½" x 8½" background #4 piece to the left of the *N*. Join a four-unit flying-geese strip to the left of this unit. Make sure it is pointing upward. Sew a 1½" x 8½" background #4 strip to each side of the Pear block that was made with background #4. Sew a flying-geese unit, pointing downward, to the right of the Pear block. Then join this unit to the *N* block as shown.

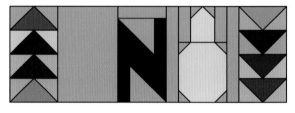

Row 4

4. For row 5, stitch the remaining 1½" x 3½" background #5 piece to the top of the *T* block. Then sew the 1½" x 8½" background #5 strip to the left of the *T* block and the 3½" x 8½" background #5 piece to the right of the *T*. Select the Pear block made with background #5 and join it to the left of the *T*. Sew a flying-geese strip to the right of the *T*, making sure it is pointing downward.

To complete the row, sew a 4½" x 8½" background #1 piece to the Pear block. Finally, join one of the Pear blocks made with background #1 to this end of the row.

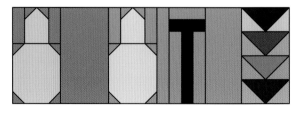

Row 5

5. For row 6, sew the remaining 1½" x 3½" background #1 piece above the letter *Y* block. Sew a flying-geese unit to the right side of the *Y* block, pointing downward. Sew the remaining 4½" x 8½" background #1 piece to the top of the remaining flying-geese unit, which should be pointing to the left. Join this section to the left of the *Y* block. To complete the row, sew the remaining two Pear blocks together side by side. Sew them to the left end of the row.

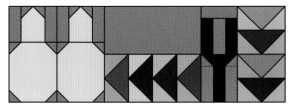

Row 6

6. Join all rows in order referring to the quilt photo on page 49 and the quilt plan at right.

Appliqué

Using the patterns on page 54, prepare four pears, nine leaves, a bowl, and a bowl rim for appliqué. We used fusible appliqué and then stitched around the shapes with a machine blanket stitch. Refer to "Appliqué" on page 7 for more information.

1. Referring to the color photograph for placement, appliqué the pears, leaves, bowl, and rim in place.

2. Cut nine pear stems, each ¼" x 1", from the brown wool. Position the stems at the top of the pears (including the pieced pears) and stitch them in place by machine. We used a double-overlock stitch. If your machine does not have this stitch, a blanket stitch would work.

Adding the Borders

For each step, press all seam allowances toward the newly added border.

1. Sew the 23½"-long red plaid strips to the top and bottom of the quilt.

2. Piece the remaining three red plaid strips together end to end to make one long strip. From this strip, cut two strips 50½" long and sew them to the sides of the quilt.

3. For the outer border, sew the 25½"-long brown print strips to the top and bottom of the quilt.

4. Piece the remaining three brown print strips together end to end to form one long strip. From this strip, cut two strips 55½" long and stitch them to the sides of the quilt.

Quilt plan

Finishing

Layer the quilt top, batting, and backing. Baste the layers together and quilt as desired. In the quilt shown, the letters were quilted in the ditch. The pears were quilted with long ovals, echoing the shape of the pears. The background triangles of the flying-geese units were quilted ¼" from the seam lines. The remaining background areas were quilted with a small stipple and the outer border was quilted with a continuous leaf shape. Bind the quilt using the 1½" brown print strips, referring to page 9 for more information.

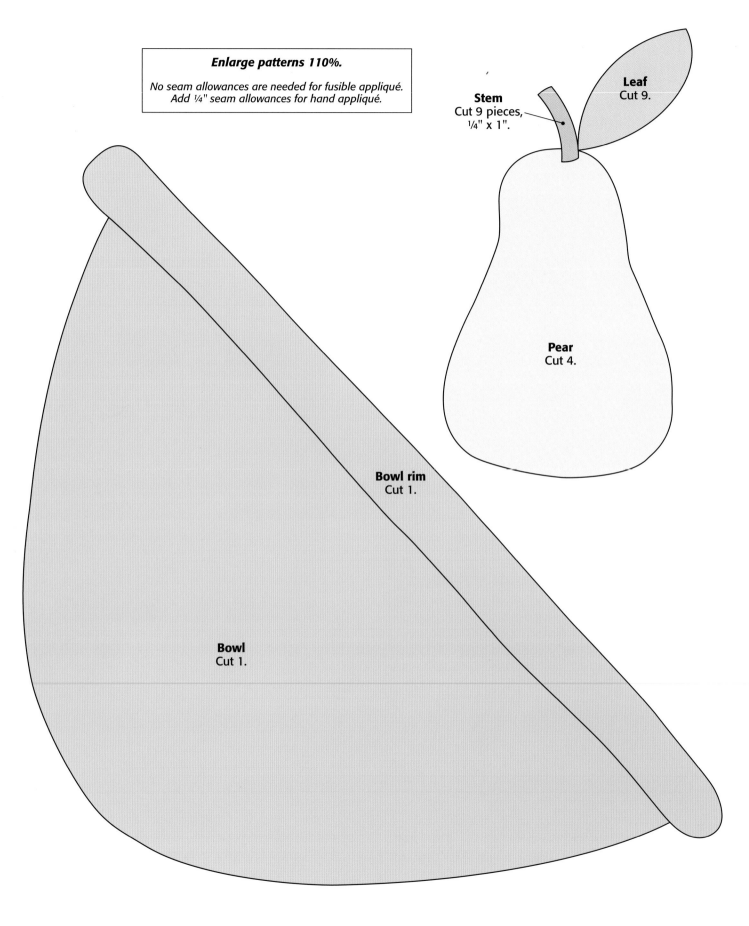

Enlarge patterns 110%.

No seam allowances are needed for fusible appliqué.
Add ¼" seam allowances for hand appliqué.

Leaf
Cut 9.

Stem
Cut 9 pieces,
¼" x 1".

Pear
Cut 4.

Bowl rim
Cut 1.

Bowl
Cut 1.

Pear

Quilt Size: 23" x 40"

I love pears! Bartlett, Anjou, Bosc—they're all delicious. Not only do I enjoy eating them, I also like collecting them. I have some great carved wooden pears displayed in a beautiful pewter bowl. Even my flower garden sports a large concrete pear. From the graceful shape to the wonderful color array of the ripening fruit, pears are amazing. And since I also love anything patriotic, a flag just seemed to fit with my extra-large pear.

~Avis

Materials

Yardage is based on 42"-wide fabric.
1⅛ yards of tan stripe for background
⅝ yard of green print for pear
⅝ yard of red plaid for flag
⅓ yard of khaki solid for letter backgrounds
¼ yard of black stripe for letters
¼ yard of cream solid for flag
¼ yard of red-and-blue plaid for spacer blocks
¼ yard of blue print for Churn Dash blocks
⅛ yard of dark blue print for flag star field
⅛ yard of brown print for flagpole
Scrap of brown print for pear stem
¼ yard of dark blue print for binding*
1⅝ yards of backing fabric
29" x 46" piece of batting

*Yardage is sufficient for single-fold binding. Buy ⅓ yard for double-fold binding.

Cutting

Refer to "The Alphabet" on page 11 for cutting the pieces needed for the letters and letter backgrounds.

From the tan stripe, cut:
- ✦ 1 piece, 17½" x 33½"
- ✦ 6 squares, 2⅞" x 2⅞"; cut the squares in half once diagonally to yield 12 triangles
- ✦ 6 pieces, 1½" x 2½"
- ✦ 6 pieces, 1½" x 3½"
- ✦ 3 pieces, 2½" x 3½"

From the black stripe, cut:
- ✦ Pieces needed for the letters *(PEAR)*

From the khaki solid, cut:
- ✦ Pieces needed for the letter backgrounds *(PEAR)*
- ✦ 2 strips, 1½" x 42"; crosscut into the following lengths:
  - 2 pieces, 1½" x 3½"
  - 3 pieces, 1½" x 5½"
  - 1 piece, 1½" x 7½"
  - 1 strip, 1½" x 33½"
- ✦ 1 strip, 2½" x 42"; crosscut into the following lengths:
  - 1 strip, 2½" x 15½"
  - 1 piece, 2½" x 8½"

From the blue print for Churn Dash blocks, cut:
- ✦ 6 squares, 2⅞" x 2⅞"; cut the squares in half once diagonally to yield 12 triangles
- ✦ 6 pieces, 1½" x 2½"
- ✦ 6 pieces, 1½" x 3½"

From the red-and-blue plaid, cut:
- ✦ 3 pieces, 1½" x 7½"
- ✦ 1 piece, 2½" x 7½"

From the dark blue print for binding, cut:
- ✦ 4 strips, 1½" x 42" (for *single-fold* binding)

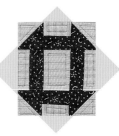

Appliqué

Using the patterns on pages 59 and 60, prepare the pear for your favorite method of appliqué. We used invisible machine appliqué for the pear because we felt that the shape was too large to use fusible appliqué—it would make the quilt too stiff. Refer to page 8 for instructions on this method. Also prepare the pear stem, flag piece, flag stripes, and star field for appliqué. We fused these shapes and blanket-stitched around them by machine for a decorative touch.

1. Appliqué the pear onto the large tan stripe rectangle, centering it horizontally and placing it approximately 1½" from the bottom raw edge of the rectangle. Tuck the stem under the pear before finishing the appliqué at the top of the pear. Complete the stem appliqué, too.

2. For the flag, it is helpful to mark the flagpole placement first. This will ensure the proper angle for the flag. Position the red plaid flag piece first, then appliqué the cream-colored stripes onto the flag. Add the dark blue print star field to complete the flag. Finally, add the brown print flagpole. The pole should slightly overlap the flag. Refer to the color photograph on page 55 for placement.

Piecing the Letters

Press the seam allowances toward the background pieces whenever possible.

1. Piece the letter blocks needed for the word *PEAR* referring to "The Alphabet" on page 11. Use the black stripe for the letters and the khaki for the letter backgrounds.

2. Sew a 1½" x 3½" khaki piece to the bottom of the *P* block. Then sew the *E* block below this unit. Join the 2½" x 15½" khaki strip to the right side of the unit and then attach 1½" x 5½" khaki strips to the top and bottom of the unit.

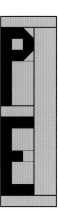

3. Sew the 1½" x 7½" khaki piece to the right side of the *A* block. Sew the remaining 1½" x 3½" khaki piece to the top of the *R* block. Attach the 2½" x 8½" khaki strip to the right of the *R* and then sew it to the bottom of the *A* block. Sew the remaining 1½" x 5½" khaki strip to the bottom of the *R* unit.

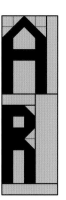

4. Sew the *PE* unit to the top of the *AR* unit and then join the 1½" x 33½" khaki strip to the left of this unit. Join this unit to the left of the pear appliqué rectangle.

Piecing the Churn Dash Blocks

1. Sew the blue and tan triangles together to make 12 triangle squares. Press the seam allowances toward the blue fabric.

Make 12.

2. Stitch together the 1½" x 2½" blue and tan pieces along their long edges. In the same manner, sew the 1½" x 3½" blue and tan pieces together. Make six of each.

Make 6 of each.

3. Stitch the units from steps 1 and 2 together along with a 2½" x 3½" tan piece to form a Churn Dash block as shown. Make three.

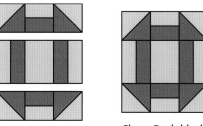

Churn Dash block.
Make 3.

Assembling the Quilt Top

1. Join the three Churn Dash blocks in a horizontal row, separating them with the 1½" x 7½" red-and-blue plaid strips. Also sew one of these strips to the right end of the row. Add the 2½" x 7½" plaid strip to the left end of the row.

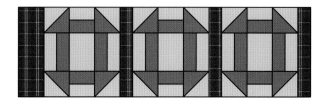

2. Sew the completed Churn Dash block row to the bottom of the quilt top.

Finishing

Layer the quilt top, batting, and backing. Baste the layers together and quilt as desired. In the quilt shown, the background of the letters was machine quilted with a meandering stitch. The Churn Dash blocks were outline quilted. The pear was echo quilted and the pear background was quilted by following the stripes in the fabric to make a brick pattern. Bind the quilt using the 1½" dark blue print strips, referring to page 9 for more information.

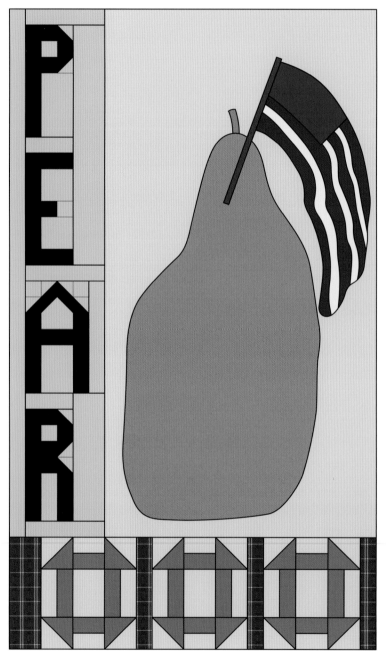

Quilt plan

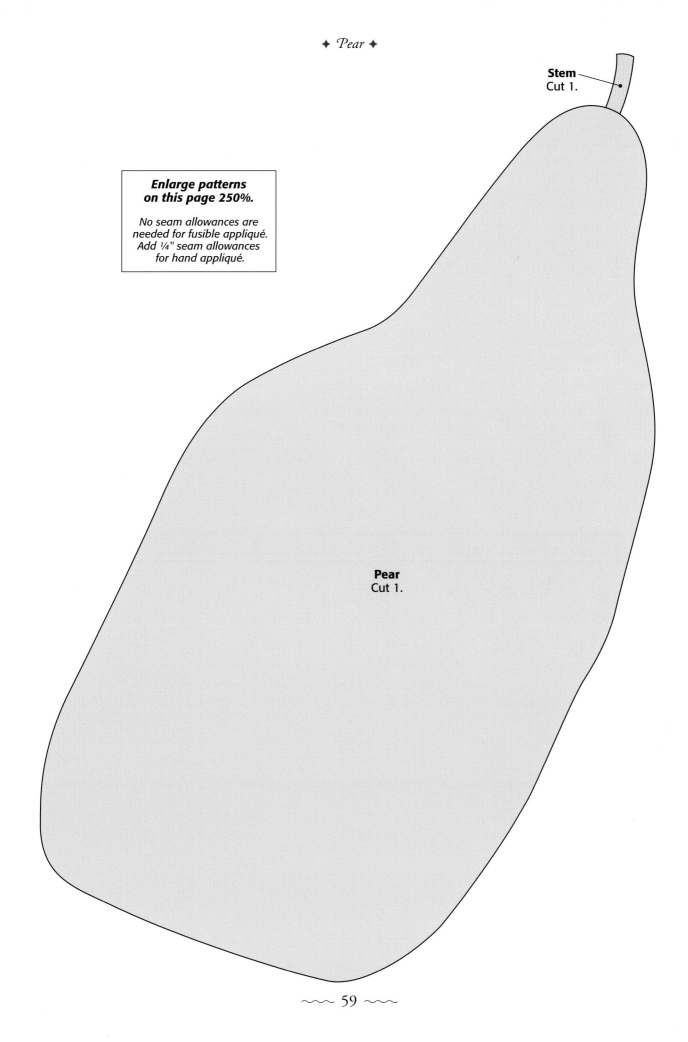

Stem
Cut 1.

Enlarge patterns on this page 250%.

No seam allowances are needed for fusible appliqué. Add ¼" seam allowances for hand appliqué.

Pear
Cut 1.

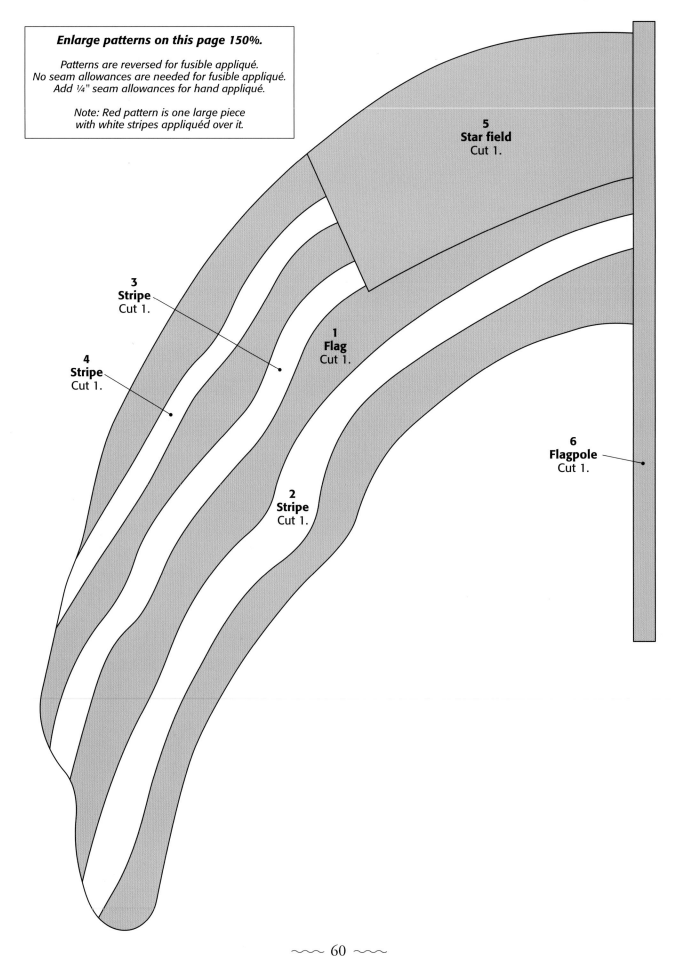

Enlarge patterns on this page 150%.

Patterns are reversed for fusible appliqué.
No seam allowances are needed for fusible appliqué.
Add ¼" seam allowances for hand appliqué.

Note: Red pattern is one large piece
with white stripes appliquéd over it.

5
Star field
Cut 1.

3
Stripe
Cut 1.

1
Flag
Cut 1.

4
Stripe
Cut 1.

6
Flagpole
Cut 1.

2
Stripe
Cut 1.

Pineapple

Quilt Size: 29" x 46"

In this quilt, we combined three of our favorite things: pineapples, Log Cabin blocks, and Shoo Fly blocks. We added a little twist by stretching the Shoo Fly blocks into tall rectangles and by turning elongated Log Cabin blocks into golden pineapples instead of piecing the traditional Pineapple variation of the Log Cabin block.
- Tammy

Materials

Yardage is based on 42"-wide fabric.

⅝ yard of black stripe for outer border

½ yard of maroon-and-tan print for letter backgrounds

⅜ yard of black-and-green check for letters

⅜ yard of maroon check for Pineapple blocks

⅜ yard of tan print for Shoo Fly blocks

⅜ yard of green check for inner border and pineapple-top appliqué

¼ yard *each* of 4 assorted maroon prints, plaids, or stripes for Shoo Fly blocks

¼ yard *each* of 2 green prints or plaids for pineapple-top appliqués

⅛ yard *each* of 11 assorted gold prints, plaids, or stripes for Pineapple blocks

¼ yard of black print for binding*

1⅝ yards of backing fabric

35" x 52" piece of batting

*Yardage is sufficient for single-fold binding. Buy ⅓ yard for double-fold binding.

Cutting

Refer to "The Alphabet" on page 11 for cutting the pieces needed for the letters and letter backgrounds.

From the black-and-green check, cut:
✦ Pieces needed for the letters *(PINEAPPLE)*

From the maroon-and-tan print, cut:
✦ Pieces needed for the letter backgrounds *(PINEAPPLE)*
✦ 1 strip, 1½" x 40½"
✦ 1 strip, 1½" x 31½"
✦ 2 strips, 1½" x 22½"
✦ 5 pieces, 1½" x 7½"
✦ 2 pieces, 1½" x 4½"
✦ 3 pieces, 1½" x 3½"

From the tan print, cut:
✦ 8 squares, 2⅞" x 2⅞"; cut the squares in half once diagonally to yield 16 triangles
✦ 8 pieces, 2½" x 6½"
✦ 8 squares, 2½" x 2½"

From *each* of the maroon prints, plaids, or stripes, cut:
✦ 2 squares, 2⅞" x 2⅞"; cut the squares in half once diagonally to yield 4 triangles (16 total)
✦ 1 piece, 2½" x 6½" (4 total)

From the assorted gold prints, plaids, or stripes, cut*:
✦ 5 centers, 1½" x 3½"
✦ 20 pieces, 1" x 3½"
✦ 10 pieces, 1" x 2½"
✦ 10 pieces, 1" x 4½"
✦ 10 pieces, 1" x 5½"
✦ 10 pieces, 1½" x 4½"

*Except for the 5 center pieces, cut the pieces in pairs so that you will have matching pieces to use on opposite sides of the Log Cabin blocks.

From the maroon check, cut:
✦ 5 pieces, 3½" x 6½"
✦ 10 pieces, 1½" x 7½"
✦ 20 squares, 1½" x 1½"
✦ 1 strip, 1½" x 18½"

From the green check, cut:
✦ 2 inner-border strips, 1" x 23½"
✦ 2 inner-border strips, 1" x 41½"*

*If your fabric is not at least 41½" wide, you will need to cut an additional 1½"-wide strip and piece the inner-border strips to be long enough for your quilt.

From the black stripe, cut:
✦ 4 outer-border strips, 3" x 42"

From the black print, cut:
✦ 4 binding strips, 1½" x 42" (for *single-fold* binding)

Piecing the Letters

1. Piece the letter blocks needed for the word *PINEAPPLE* referring to "The Alphabet" on page 11. Use the black-and-green check for the letters and the maroon-and-tan print for the letter backgrounds.

2. Stitch together the *P, I, N, E,* and *A* blocks with the five 1½" x 7½" maroon-and-tan print pieces as shown. Stitch the 1½" x 22½" background strips to the top and bottom of this unit.

3. Sew the *P, P, L,* and *E* blocks together vertically, separating them with the three 1½" x 3½" maroon-and-tan strips. Add the 1½" x 31½" maroon-and-tan strip to the left side of this unit.

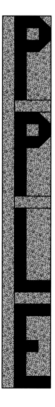

Piecing the Shoo Fly Blocks

1. Stitch together the 2⅞" tan and maroon triangles to make 16 triangle squares.

2. Lay out four matching triangle squares, a matching 2½" x 6½" maroon piece, two 2½" tan squares, and two 2½" x 6½" tan rectangles as shown. Sew the pieces together in rows and then sew the rows together to complete the block. Repeat to make a total of four Shoo Fly blocks. The blocks should measure 6½" x 10½", including seam allowances.

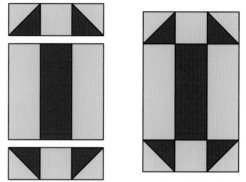

Shoo Fly block.
Make 4.

Piecing the Pineapple Blocks

Piece five Pineapple blocks. Use the assorted gold pieces to make the center Log Cabins. The blocks are finished with the maroon check pieces.

1. Stitch two matching 1" x 3½" gold strips to opposite long sides of a 1½" x 3½" gold center piece. Press the seam allowances here and throughout toward the newly added pieces. Add a pair of 1" x 2½" pieces to the top and bottom of the block to complete round 1.

2. For round 2, sew matching 1" x 4½" pieces to the long sides of the block. Then attach matching 1" x 3½" pieces to the top and bottom of the block.

3. Round 3 is completed in the same manner, using a set of matching 1" x 5½" pieces on the sides of the block and 1½" x 4½" pieces on the top and bottom.

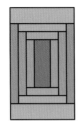

4. Using the folded-corner technique on page 7, place a 1½" maroon check square on one corner of the unit and stitch, trim, and press. Repeat on all four corners of the pieced block.

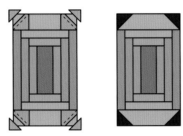

5. Sew 1½" x 7½" maroon check pieces to the long sides of the block. To complete the block, sew a 3½" x 6½" maroon check piece to the top of the block. Repeat all the steps to complete five Pineapple blocks. Your finished blocks should measure 6½" x 10½", including the seam allowances.

Pineapple block.
Make 5.

Assembling the Quilt Top

1. Lay out the Pineapple and Shoo Fly blocks in three rows of three blocks each. The Pineapple blocks should be in the four corners and center of the arrangement. Stitch the blocks together in rows and then sew the rows together. Sew the 1½" x 18½" maroon check strip to the bottom of the quilt top.

2. Add the *PINE* word unit to the top of the quilt top. Then add the *APPLE* word unit to the right side of the quilt top referring to the quilt plan, opposite. Attach the 1½" x 40½" maroon-and-tan strip to the right side of the quilt top.

3. Using the pineapple-top pattern on page 65, prepare five pineapple tops for your favorite method of appliqué. We used fusible appliqué, reversing the template for three of the blocks. We used a machine blanket stitch to finish the edges of the appliqués. Refer to "Appliqué" on page 7 for more information. Note that the tip of the pineapple top will lie on the block above it. Refer to the quilt photograph on page 61 for placement.

4. Sew the 1" x 23½" green check strips to the top and bottom of the quilt top. Sew the 1" x 41½" green check strips to the sides of the quilt. Press all seam allowances toward the borders.

5. For the outer border, trim two of the 3"-wide black stripe strips to 24½" long and stitch them to the top and bottom of the quilt top. Sew the leftover piece from each of these strips to one of the remaining 3"-wide black stripe strips. From these long strips, cut two side borders 46½" long. Sew them to the sides of the quilt top. Press the seam allowances toward the outer borders.

Finishing

Layer the quilt top, batting, and backing. Baste the layers together and quilt as desired. In the quilt shown, the Pineapple blocks were echo quilted and arcs were quilted in the Shoo Fly blocks. The letters were quilted in the ditch and the background was stippled. Bind the quilt using the 1½" black print strips, referring to page 9 for more information.

Quilt plan

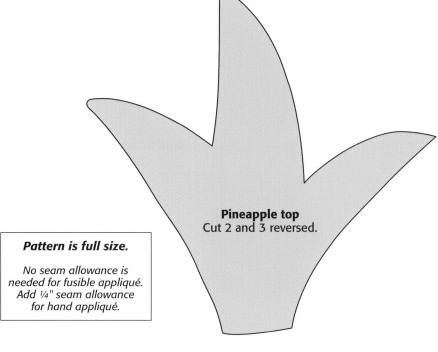

Pineapple top
Cut 2 and 3 reversed.

Pattern is full size.

*No seam allowance is
needed for fusible appliqué.
Add ¼" seam allowance
for hand appliqué.*

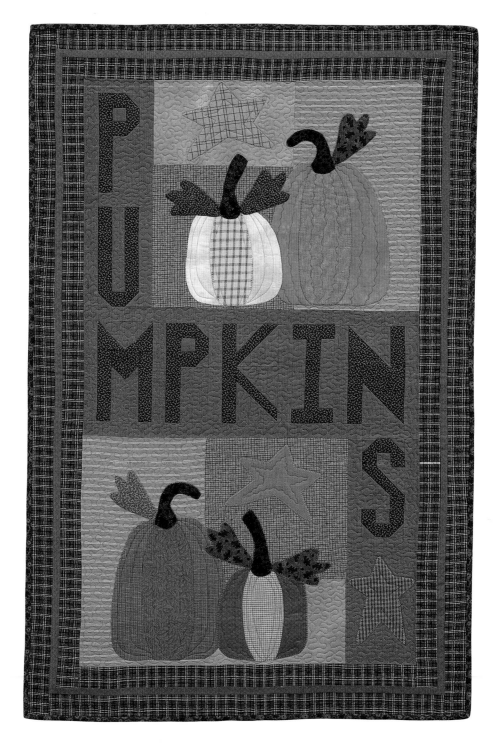

Pumpkins

Quilt Size: 31" x 48"

*My favorite part of autumn is the wonderful array of colors that Mother Nature provides.
I enjoy decorating the front of the house with colorful chrysanthemums and pumpkins of all
shapes and sizes. Add a creamy white pumpkin to the mix and the decorating is complete.*
~ Tammy

Materials

Yardage is based on 42"-wide fabric.

⅝ yard of green plaid for inner and outer borders
⅝ yard of olive drab for letter backgrounds
½ yard *each* of 6 orange prints or plaids for pumpkin appliqués
⅓ yard *each* of 2 khaki plaids or stripes (#1 and #2) for appliqué backgrounds
⅜ yard of orange-and-green print for letters
⅜ yard *each* of 2 cream prints or plaids for pumpkin appliqués
¼ yard of khaki plaid or stripe (#3) for appliqué background
¼ yard *each* of 3 gold prints, plaids, or solids for star appliqués
¼ yard *each* of 3 greens for leaf appliqués
¼ yard *each* of 2 browns for stem appliqués
¼ yard of orange print for middle border
¼ yard of olive green print for binding*
1¾ yards of backing fabric
37" x 54" piece of batting

Yardage is sufficient for single-fold binding. Buy ⅜ yard for double-fold binding.

Cutting

Refer to "The Alphabet" on page 11 for cutting the pieces needed for the letters and letter backgrounds.

From the orange-and-green print, cut:
✦ Pieces needed for the letters (*PUMPKINS*)

From the olive drab, cut:
✦ Pieces needed for the letter backgrounds (*PUMPKINS*)
✦ 1 piece, 5½" x 9½"
✦ 2 strips, 1½" x 24½"
✦ 2 strips, 1½" x 16½"
✦ 8 pieces, 1½" x 7½"
✦ 2 pieces, 1½" x 3½"

From khaki #1, cut:
✦ 2 pieces, 9½" x 16½"

From khaki #2, cut:
✦ 2 squares, 10½" x 10½"

From khaki #3, cut:
✦ 2 pieces, 6½" x 10½"

From the green plaid, cut:
✦ 8 border strips, 2" x 42"

From the orange print for middle border, cut:
✦ 4 border strips, 1" x 42"

From the olive green print, cut:
✦ 5 binding strips, 1½" x 42" (for *single-fold* binding)

Piecing the Letters

1. Piece the letter blocks needed for the word *PUMPKINS* referring to "The Alphabet" on page 11. Use the orange-and-green print for the letters and the olive drab for the backgrounds.

2. Stitch the 1½" x 3½" olive drab pieces to the tops of the *P* and *U* blocks. Stitch these blocks together as shown and then sew the 1½" x 16½" olive drab strips to both sides of the unit.

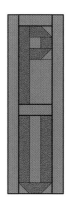

3. Now stitch together the *M, P, K, I,* and *N* blocks in a horizontal row, sewing 1½" x 7½" olive drab pieces between the letters and at each end of the row as shown. Add the 1½" x 24½" olive drab strips to the top and bottom of this row.

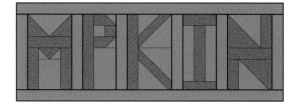

4. Sew the remaining two 1½" x 7½" olive drab strips to the sides of the *S* block. Then add the 5½" x 9½" olive drab rectangle to the bottom of this unit. Set the units aside.

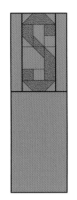

Appliqué

Using the patterns on pages 70–72, prepare the pieces for two large pumpkins, two small pumpkins, two of each stem, and six leaves. For the large and small pumpkins, cut the entire pumpkin shape from one fabric, and then cut the center pumpkin accent shape from another fabric.

1. Sew the khaki pieces together to make two large background pieces as shown.

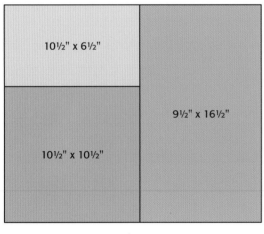

Make 2.

2. Using your favorite method, appliqué the large pumpkin shapes, large pumpkin accent shapes, small pumpkin shapes, and small pumpkin accent shapes to the pieced backgrounds. Notice that we rotated the background blocks: For one block the long background rectangle is on the right and for the other one it is on the left.

Add two leaves to each small pumpkin and one leaf to each large pumpkin. Then add the curved stems to the large pumpkins and the straight stems to the small pumpkins, reversing each of the templates for one. Finally, appliqué a star #1 above each small pumpkin. Refer to the color photograph on page 66 for placement help. We used fusible appliqué and a machine blanket stitch to finish the edges. Refer to "Appliqué" on page 7 for more information.

Make 1 of each.

3. Appliqué star #2 onto the olive drab space below the *S* block.

Assembling the Quilt Top

1. Stitch the *PU* unit to the left of the appliqué unit that has the large pumpkin on the right.

2. Stitch the remaining appliqué unit to the left of the *S* block.

3. Stitch these two units and the *MPKIN* unit together, referring to the quilt plan, opposite.

4. For the inner border, trim two of the green plaid strips to 24½" long. Sew them to the top and bottom of the quilt top. Sew the remainder of each of those strips to another green plaid strip. Then trim these two longer strips to 44½" long and sew them to the sides of the quilt top. Press all seam allowances toward the border.

5. For the middle border, trim two of the orange print strips to 27½" long. Stitch them to the top and bottom of the quilt top. Sew the remainder of each of those strips to another orange strip. Trim these two longer strips to 45½" long and sew them to the sides of the quilt top. Press all seams toward the orange border.

6. For the outer border, trim two of the green plaid strips to 28½" long. Sew them to the top and bottom of the quilt top. Sew the remainder of each of those strips to another green plaid strip. Trim these two longer strips to 48½" long and stitch them to the sides of the quilt top. Press.

Finishing

Layer the quilt top, batting, and backing. Baste the layers together and quilt as desired. In the quilt shown, the background was stipple quilted. The letters were quilted in the ditch. The stars were echo quilted and the pumpkins were quilted by echoing the center pumpkin shape. Bind the quilt using the 1½"-wide olive green print strips, referring to page 9 for more information.

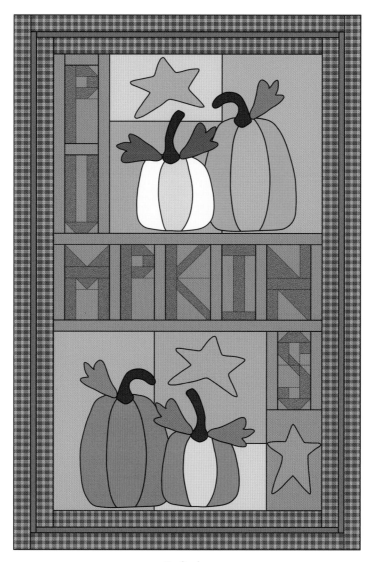

Quilt plan

Enlarge patterns on this page 125%.

Patterns are reversed for fusible appliqué.
No seam allowances are needed for fusible appliqué.
Add ¼" seam allowances for hand appliqué.

Note: Pumpkin is one large piece
with accent appliquéd over it.

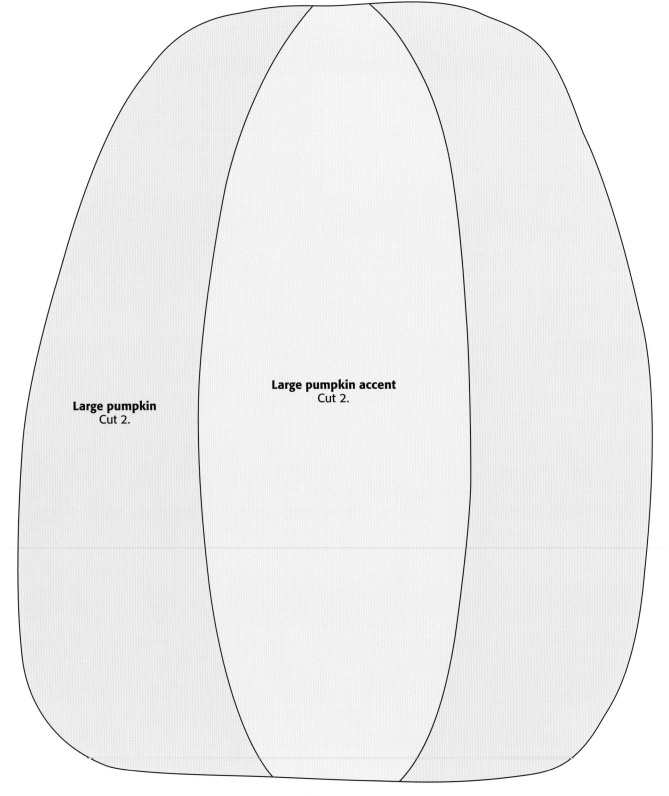

Large pumpkin accent
Cut 2.

Large pumpkin
Cut 2.

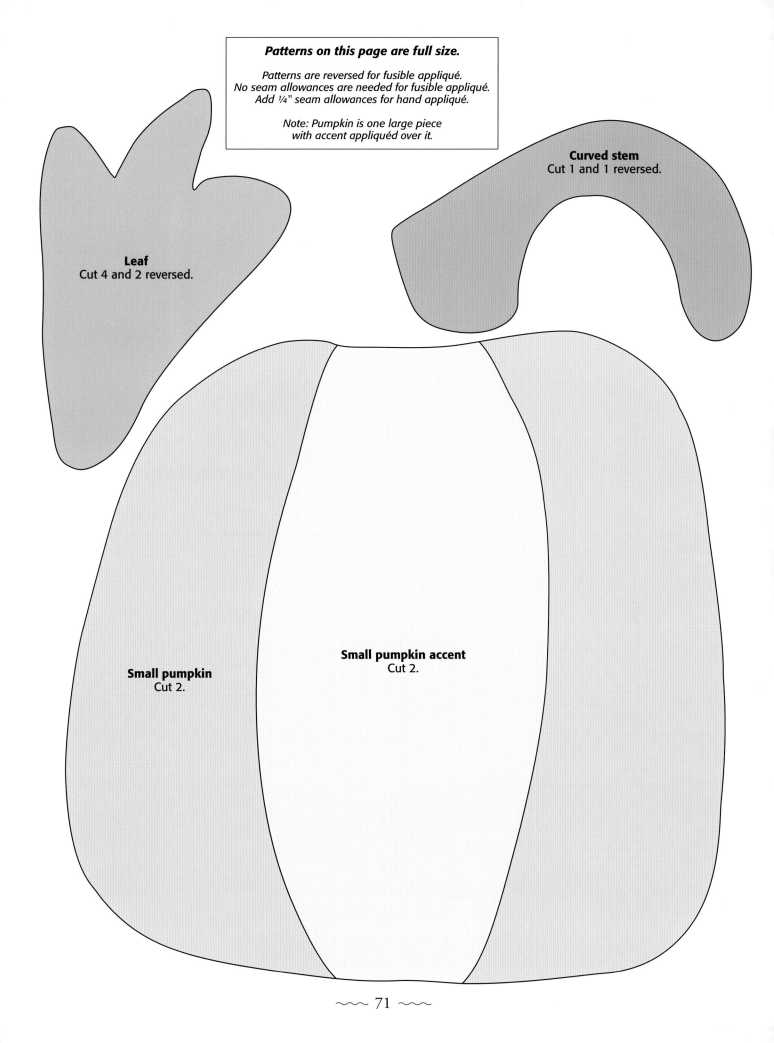

Patterns on this page are full size.

Patterns are reversed for fusible appliqué.
No seam allowances are needed for fusible appliqué.
Add ¼" seam allowances for hand appliqué.

Note: Pumpkin is one large piece
with accent appliquéd over it.

Leaf
Cut 4 and 2 reversed.

Curved stem
Cut 1 and 1 reversed.

Small pumpkin
Cut 2.

Small pumpkin accent
Cut 2.

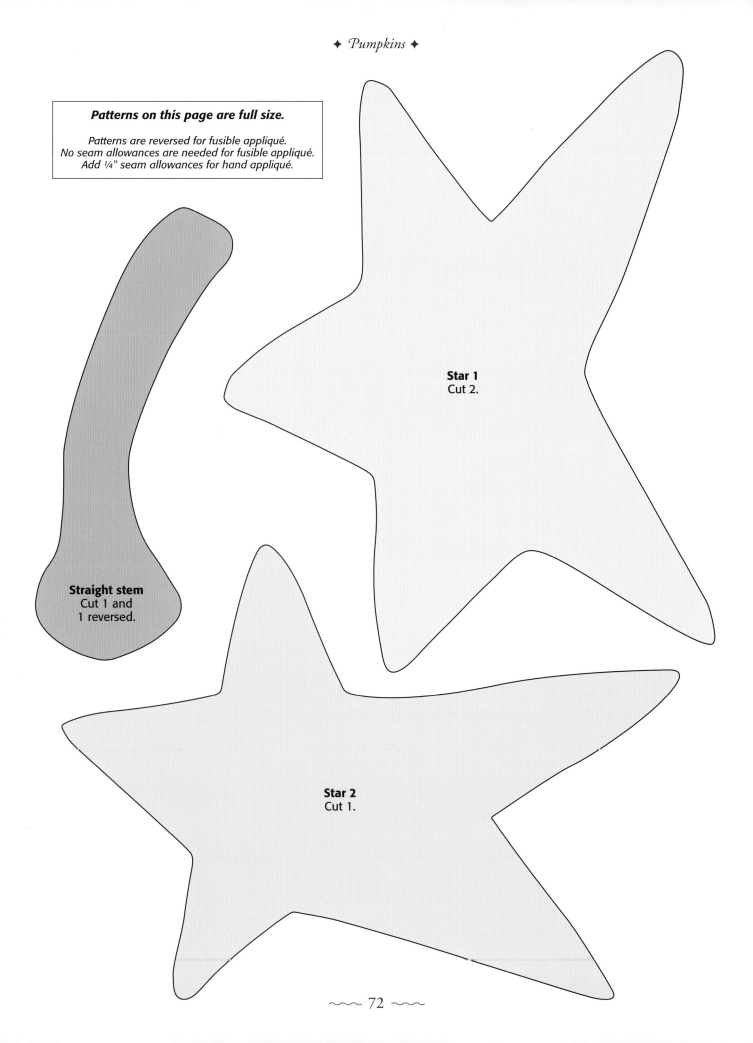

Patterns on this page are full size.

Patterns are reversed for fusible appliqué.
No seam allowances are needed for fusible appliqué.
Add ¼" seam allowances for hand appliqué.

Straight stem
Cut 1 and
1 reversed.

Star 1
Cut 2.

Star 2
Cut 1.

Red Tulips

Quilt Size: 26" x 48"

*Nothing is more showy in a spring garden than large red tulips. In my garden
I have bright red ones planted together with a burgundy variety that is almost black—
just like in this quilt. Tulip time is a short season, but this quilt will bloom all year long.*
~Avis

Materials

Yardage is based on 42"-wide fabric.

1⅛ yard of green solid for tulip backgrounds

¾ yard of tan print for letter and Churn Dash backgrounds

⅜ yard of red plaid for side borders

¼ yard *each* of 3 red prints (#1, #2, and #3) for tulips

¼ yard of red stripe for Churn Dash blocks

¼ yard of navy print for letters

¼ yard *each* of 2 olive greens (#1 and #2) for tulip stems and leaves

¼ yard of burgundy print for binding*

1¾ yards of backing fabric

32" x 54" piece of batting

Yardage is sufficient for single-fold binding. Buy ⅜ yard for double-fold binding.

Cutting

Refer to "The Alphabet" on page 11 for cutting the pieces needed for the letters and letter backgrounds.

From the navy print, cut:
✦ Pieces needed for the letters *(RED TULIPS)*

From the tan print, cut:
✦ Pieces needed for the letter backgrounds *(RED TULIPS)*
✦ 1 strip, 7½" x 42"; crosscut into:
    7 pieces, 1½" x 7½"
    2 pieces, 3" x 7½"
    2 pieces, 2" x 7½"
✦ 4 strips, 1½" x 42"; crosscut into:
    4 strips, 1½" x 26½"
    6 pieces, 1½" x 3½"
    4 squares, 1½" x 1½"
✦ 4 squares, 2⅞" x 2⅞"; cut the squares in half once diagonally to yield 8 triangles

From the red stripe, cut:
✦ 4 pieces, 1½" x 3½"
✦ 4 squares, 1½" x 1½"
✦ 4 squares, 2⅞" x 2⅞"; cut the squares in half once diagonally to yield 8 triangles

From red print #1, cut:
✦ 1 square, 1⅞" x 1⅞"; cut the square in half once diagonally to yield 2 triangles
✦ 1 piece, 1½" x 2½"
✦ 1 piece, 4½" x 8½"

From the green solid, cut:
✦ 1 piece, 14½" x 18½"
✦ 2 strips, 1½" x 42";
  crosscut into:
    2 strips, 1½" x 16½"
    2 pieces, 1½" x 9½"
    1 piece, 1½" x 6½"
    2 pieces, 1½" x 2½"
    8 squares, 1½" x 1½"
✦ 1 strip, 5½" x 42";
  crosscut into:
    1 piece, 5½" x 7½"
    1 square, 5½" x 5½"
    1 piece, 2½" x 5½"
✦ 1 piece, 4½" x 6½"
✦ 4 squares, 2½" x 2½"
✦ 2 squares, 1⅞" x 1⅞"; cut the squares in half once diagonally to yield 4 triangles

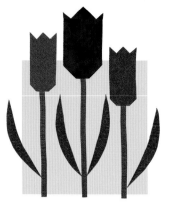

From red print #2, cut:
✦ 2 squares, 1½" x 1½"
✦ 1 piece, 2½" x 4½"
✦ 1 piece, 6½" x 9½"

From red print #3, cut:
✦ 1 square, 1⅞" x 1⅞"; cut the square in half once diagonally to yield 2 triangles
✦ 1 piece, 1½" x 2½"
✦ 1 piece, 4½" x 8½"

From the red plaid, cut:
✦ 2 strips, 4½" x 30½"

From olive green #1, cut:
✦ 2 strips, 2" x 42"

From the burgundy print, cut:
✦ 5 binding strips, 1½" x 42" (for *single-fold* binding)

Piecing the Letters

1. Piece the letter blocks needed for the words *RED TULIPS* referring to "The Alphabet" on page 11. Use the navy print for the letters and the tan print for the backgrounds.

2. Sew the *R, E,* and *D* blocks together, separating the letters with two 1½" x 7½" tan strips as shown. Sew a 3" x 7½" tan piece to each end of

the row. Press all seam allowances toward the tan print pieces. Set aside.

3. Sew the *T, U, L, I, P,* and *S* blocks together, separating them with the remaining 1½" x 7½" tan strips. Sew a 2" x 7½" tan strip to each end of the row. To complete the row, sew a 1½" x 26½" tan strip to the top and bottom. Press all seam allowances toward the tan print pieces.

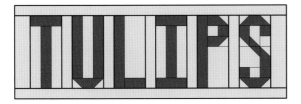

Piecing the Churn Dash Blocks

1. Sew the 1½" x 3½" red stripe and tan print pieces together in pairs. Also sew the 1½" red stripe and tan print squares together in pairs. Make four of each unit. Press the seam allowances toward the red fabric.

Make 4 of each.

2. Stitch the 2⅞" red stripe and tan print triangles together to make eight triangle squares. Press the seam allowances toward the red stripe fabric.

3. Lay out the units and the remaining 1½" x 3½" tan pieces as shown. Sew them together in rows,

and then sew the rows together to make two Churn Dash blocks.

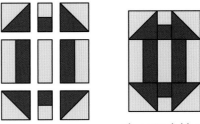

Churn Dash block.
Make 2.

4. Join a Churn Dash block to each end of the *RED* unit. To complete the row, sew a 26½"-long tan strip to the top and bottom of the row.

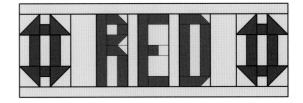

Piecing the Tulips

The tulips are made in the same manner, but each one uses slightly different-sized pieces and a different red fabric. The left tulip uses the pieces cut from red print #1, the center tulip is made with the pieces cut from red print #2, and the right tulip uses the pieces cut from red print #3.

Left Tulip (Red Print #1)

1. Stitch together 1⅞" red print and green solid triangles to make a triangle square. Make two.

Make 2.

2. Using the folded-corner technique on page 7, sew a 1½" green square to the 1½" x 2½" red print rectangle. Trim and press as shown. Repeat on the other corner.

3. Stitch the triangle squares from step 1 to the end of the unit from step 2 as shown.

4. Using the folded-corner technique, sew 1½" green squares to the two bottom corners of the 4½" x 8½" red print rectangle.

5. Stitch the two sections together.

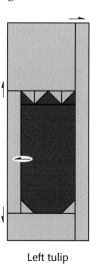

6. Complete the left tulip by first stitching a 1½" x 9½" green piece to the left of the tulip; then add the 5½" green square to the top of the tulip, the 2½" x 5½" green rectangle to the bottom of the tulip, and finally a 1½" x 16½" green strip to the right side of the unit. Press all seam allowances toward the green fabric.

Left tulip

Center Tulip (Red Print #2)

1. Using the folded-corner technique, sew a 1½" red print square to a 1½" x 2½" green piece. Trim and press as shown. Repeat to make another unit, but make sure that the stitching is angled in the opposite direction from the first one.

Make 1
of each.

2. In the same manner, stitch a 2½" green square to one end of the 2½" x 4½" red print rectangle. Trim and press. Repeat on the other end of the rectangle.

3. Stitch the units from steps 1 and 2 together.

4. Using the folded-corner technique, sew 2½" green squares to the two bottom corners of the 6½" x 9½" red print piece as shown. Sew this unit to the unit from step 3.

5. To complete the center tulip, sew the 1½" x 6½" green strip to the top of the tulip and the 4½" x 6½" green piece to the bottom of the tulip. Finally, sew the remaining 1½" x 16½" green strip to the right side of the tulip.

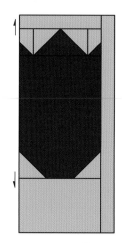

Center tulip

Right Tulip (Red Print #3)

1. Using green and red print #3 pieces, follow steps 1–5 of "Left Tulip (Red Print #1)" to piece the right tulip.

2. Complete the right tulip by stitching the remaining 1½" x 9½" green strip to the right of the tulip. Then sew the 5½" x 7½" green piece to the top of the tulip.

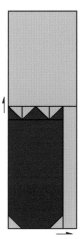

Right tulip

Assembling the Quilt Top

1. Stitch the three tulip sections together, making sure you have them in the correct order: left, center, and right.

2. Sew the 14½" x 18½" green piece to the bottom of the tulips (along the 18½" long edge). Press the seam allowance toward the background fabric.

3. Sew the 4½" x 30½" red plaid strips to the sides of the tulips. Press the seam allowances toward the red fabric.

4. Prepare the 2"-wide olive green #1 strips for the stem appliqués. From one of the strips, cut one piece 15" long and one piece 17" long. From the other 2" strip, cut one piece 19" long. Fold each strip in half lengthwise with *wrong* sides together. Stitch the long raw edges together with a ¼" seam allowance. Then use a ¾"-wide bias bar to press each strip as described on page 9.

← Bias bar

5. Appliqué the stems in place, centering each under a tulip and turning under ¼" on the short ends that butt up to the tulips. (The excess stem length at the bottom of the stem can be trimmed off after the tulip section is joined to the row below it.) We machine appliquéd the stems in place using matching thread and a blind hem stitch. Set the stitch to shorter and narrower than normal so it will be virtually invisible. Or, appliqué the stems by hand.

Using the olive green #2 fabric, prepare two leaves and two reversed leaves for fusible appliqué. Refer to the quilt photograph on page 73 for placement. The leaves are fused in place and then machine blanket-stitched with matching thread. Refer to "Appliqué" on page 7 for more information.

6. Stitch the *RED* unit to the top of the tulips and the *TULIPS* unit to the bottom of the tulips.

Quilt plan

Finishing

Layer the quilt top, batting, and backing. Baste the layers together and quilt as desired. In the quilt shown, the letters and Churn Dash blocks were outline quilted and the background was meander quilted by machine. The leaves were quilted with squiggly lines and the tulips were quilted with curved lines to echo the shape of a tulip petal. Bind the quilt using the 1½" burgundy strips, referring to page 9 for more information.

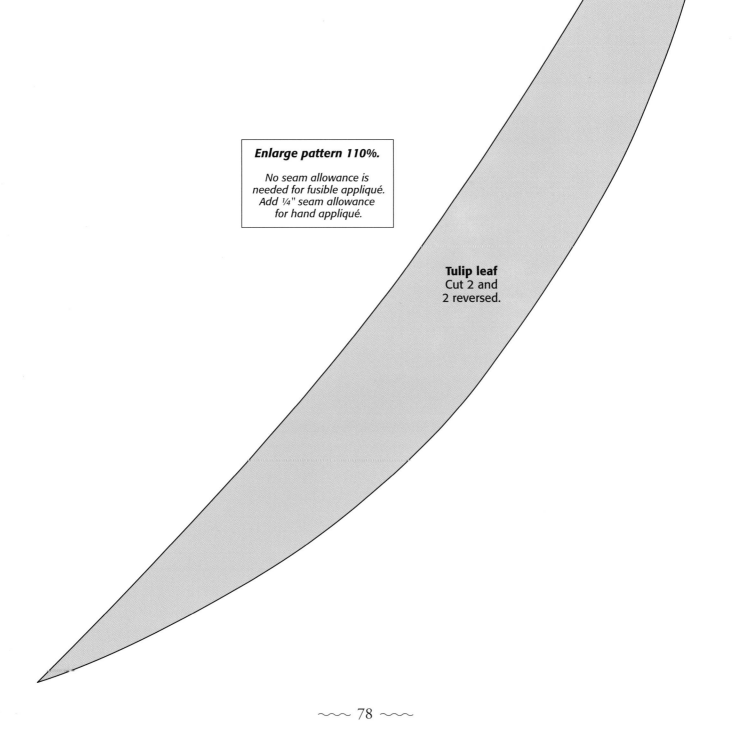

Enlarge pattern 110%.

No seam allowance is needed for fusible appliqué. Add ¼" seam allowance for hand appliqué.

Tulip leaf
Cut 2 and
2 reversed.

Snowman

Quilt Size: 29" x 52"

When I was younger, nothing was better on a cold winter day than building a snowman.
The snowman wasn't complete until I had found the perfect sticks for his arms, stones for his
eyes, and carrot for his nose. To top it off, he needed a hat and scarf to keep him warm.
- Tammy

Materials

Yardage is based on 42"-wide fabric.

¾ yard of medium blue print for letter backgrounds, middle border, and binding

⅝ yard of cream solid for snowman and letters

⅝ yard of blue stripe for borders

½ yard *each* of 6 blue plaids, prints, or stripes (#1, #2, #3, #4, #5, and #6) for background

⅜ yard *each* of 4 assorted green prints (#1, #2, #3, and #4) for tree

¼ yard of black solid for hat and eyes

⅛ yard of brown stripe for tree trunk

Scrap of brown check for stick arms

Scrap of orange for carrot nose

Scrap of white for eyes

6" x 12" piece of blue checked wool for scarf

1⅞ yards of backing fabric

35" x 58" piece of batting

Black embroidery floss

Cutting

Refer to "The Alphabet" on page 11 for cutting the pieces needed for the letters and letter backgrounds.

From the cream solid, cut:
✦ Pieces needed for the letters *(SNOWMAN)*
✦ 1 piece, 8½" x 14½"
✦ 1 piece, 6½" x 7½"
✦ 1 piece, 4½" x 5½"

From the medium blue print, cut:
✦ Pieces needed for the letter backgrounds *(SNOWMAN)*
✦ 4 strips, 1" x 42"
✦ 3 squares, 3½" x 3½"
✦ 5 binding strips, 1½" x 42"

From the assorted green prints, cut:
✦ 1 square, 7⅞" x 7⅞", from each of the four greens; cut the squares in half once diagonally to yield 8 triangles
✦ 1 piece, 4½" x 7½", from green #3
✦ 1 square, 3½" x 3½", from green #4

From blue prints #1–#4, cut:
✦ 1 square, 7⅞" x 7⅞", from each of the four blues; cut the squares in half once diagonally to yield 8 triangles

From blue print #3, cut:
✦ 1 piece, 7½" x 14½"
✦ 1 strip, 4½" x 23½"
✦ 1 piece, 4½" x 7½"
✦ 1 square, 4½" x 4½"
✦ 1 piece, 3½" x 7½"

From blue print #4, cut:
✦ 1 piece, 4½" x 7½"
✦ 1 piece, 3½" x 7½"

From blue print #5, cut:
✦ 1 piece, 2½" x 7½"
✦ 1 piece, 2½" x 4½"
✦ 3 pieces, 1½" x 7½"
✦ 12 squares, 1½" x 1½"

From blue print #6, cut:
✦ 1 piece, 4½" x 7½"
✦ 1 piece, 1½" x 7½"

From the brown stripe, cut:
✦ 1 strip, 1½" x 28½"
✦ 1 piece, 1½" x 7½"

From the blue stripe, cut:
✦ 8 strips, 1¾" x 42"

Piecing the Letters

Piece the letter blocks needed for the word *SNOW-MAN* referring to "The Alphabet" on page 11. Use the cream solid for the letters and the medium blue print for the letter backgrounds. Set the blocks aside.

Constructing the Tree Units

1. Sew the 7⅞" blue and green triangles together to make six triangle squares in the following color combinations.

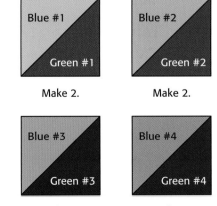

Make 2.   Make 2.

Make 1.   Make 1.

2. Using the folded-corner technique on page 7, stitch the 4½" blue #3 square to one end of the 4½" x 7½" green #3 piece as shown.

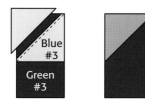

3. In the same manner, stitch the 3½" green #4 square to one end of the 3½" x 7½" blue #4 piece. Set all the tree pieces aside.

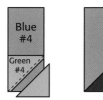

Constructing the Snowman Blocks

1. To make the snowman's base, use the folded-corner technique to join a 1½" blue #5 square to each corner of the 8½" x 14½" cream solid rectangle.

Snowman base

2. For the midsection, repeat step 1, this time sewing the 1½" blue #5 squares to each corner of the 6½" x 7½" cream solid piece. Add 1½" x 7½" blue #5 strips to opposite sides of the unit. Press the seam allowances toward the blue fabric.

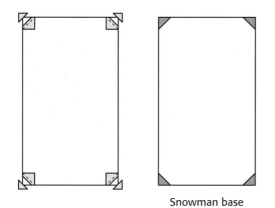

Snowman midsection

3. In the same manner, sew the remaining 1½" blue #5 squares to the corners of the 4½" x 5½" cream solid piece. Add the 2½" x 4½" blue #5 piece to the top of this unit. Add the 2½" x 7½" blue #5 piece to the left of the unit and the remaining 1½" x 7½" blue #5 piece to the right side. This completes the snowman's head. Press the seam allowances toward the blue fabric. Set all three snowman blocks aside.

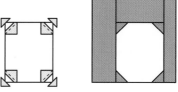

Snowman head

Assembling the Quilt Top

1. To make unit 1, sew the 4½" x 7½" blue #4 rectangle to the right of one of the *N* blocks. To the right of this unit, sew a triangle square made with green #1 and blue #1 as shown.

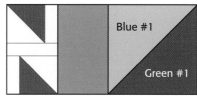

Unit 1

2. To make unit 2, sew the 4½" x 7½" blue #6 rectangle to one side of the *O* block and the 1½" x 7½" blue #6 piece to the opposite side of the *O*. Then attach a triangle square made with green #2 and blue #2 to the right end of this unit as shown.

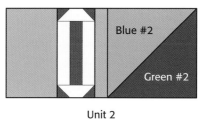

Unit 2

3. To make unit 3, stitch together the snowman's head, the *W* block, and the tree unit made with

green #3 and blue #3 in step 2 of "Constructing the Tree Units" at the top of page 81.

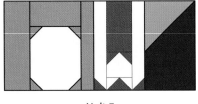

Unit 3

4. To make unit 4, stitch together the snowman's midsection, the tree unit made with green #4 and blue #4 in step 3 of "Constructing the Tree Units," and the *M* block.

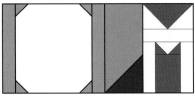

Unit 4

5. Stitch units 1–4 together in a vertical column as shown below. Add the 1½" x 28½" brown stripe strip to the right side of this unit.

6. Stitch the remaining four triangle squares into a vertical row as shown, keeping the colors in order from green #1 and blue #1 on the top to green #4 and blue #4 on the bottom. Sew this unit to the right side of the unit from step 5, and then add the 4½" x 23½" blue #3 piece to the top of the unit.

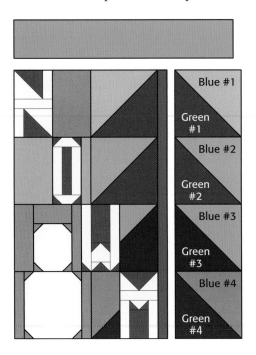

7. Stitch the 4½" x 7½" blue #3 rectangle to the right of the *A* block. Then sew together the 1½" x 7½" brown stripe piece, the 3½" x 7½" blue #3 piece, and the remaining *N* block as shown. Stitch these two units together.

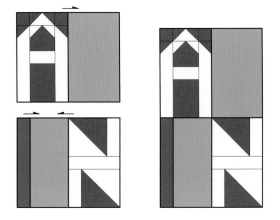

8. Sew the snowman's base and the 7½" x 14½" blue #3 rectangle together and add it to the unit from step 7.

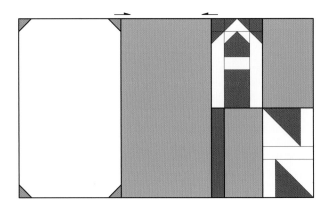

9. Stitch the snowman's base unit to the bottom of the *NOWM* section.

Adding the Borders

1. Trim four of the 1¾" x 42" blue stripe strips and two of the 1" x 42" medium blue print strips to 23½" long. (Reserve the leftovers for the side borders.) Stitch a blue stripe piece to each long side of the medium blue print strips. Press the seam allowances toward the stripe fabric. Stitch these borders to the top and bottom of the quilt top.

Make 2.

2. If your remaining 1¾" blue stripe and 1" medium blue print strips are not at least 42½" long, add the corresponding leftover strips from step 1 to make strips long enough for side borders. You'll need two blue stripe strips and one medium blue print strip that measure at least 42½" long, and two blue stripe strips and one medium blue print strip that measure at least 46½" long.

3. For the left border, stitch a 42½"-long blue stripe strip to either side of the 42½"-long medium blue print strip. Add the S block to the top of the border and a 3½" medium blue print square to the bottom of the border. Add this border to the left side of the quilt top.

Left border

4. For the right border, stitch together the three 46½"-long blue stripe and medium blue print strips. Add the remaining 3½" medium blue print squares to each end of the border and stitch it to the right side of the quilt top.

Right border

Appliqué

Using the patterns on page 84, prepare the pieces for two outer eyes, two eye centers, one nose, two arms, one hat, one hat brim, one scarf, and one scarf knot.

1. Using your favorite method, appliqué the features onto the snowman. We used fusible appliqué and a machine blanket stitch to finish the edges. Refer to "Appliqué" on page 7 for more information. Appliqué the hat and brim. Then add the nose and eyes. For the eyes, appliqué the larger white circle first. We used black thread to blanket stitch around this piece for a decorative finish. Then add the smaller black circle. Appliqué the stick arms and then add the scarf and scarf knot.

2. Using three strands of black embroidery floss, stitch six large cross-stitches for the snowman's mouth, referring to the quilt photograph on page 79 for placement.

Quilt plan

Finishing

Layer the quilt top, batting, and backing. Baste the layers together and quilt as desired. In the quilt shown, the letters were echo quilted and the background was quilted with a loopy stipple. The snowman was quilted with spirals and the tree was quilted with a wavy diagonal line. The border pieces were quilted in the ditch and stars were quilted in the cornerstone blocks. Bind the quilt using the 1½" medium blue print strips, referring to page 9 for more information.

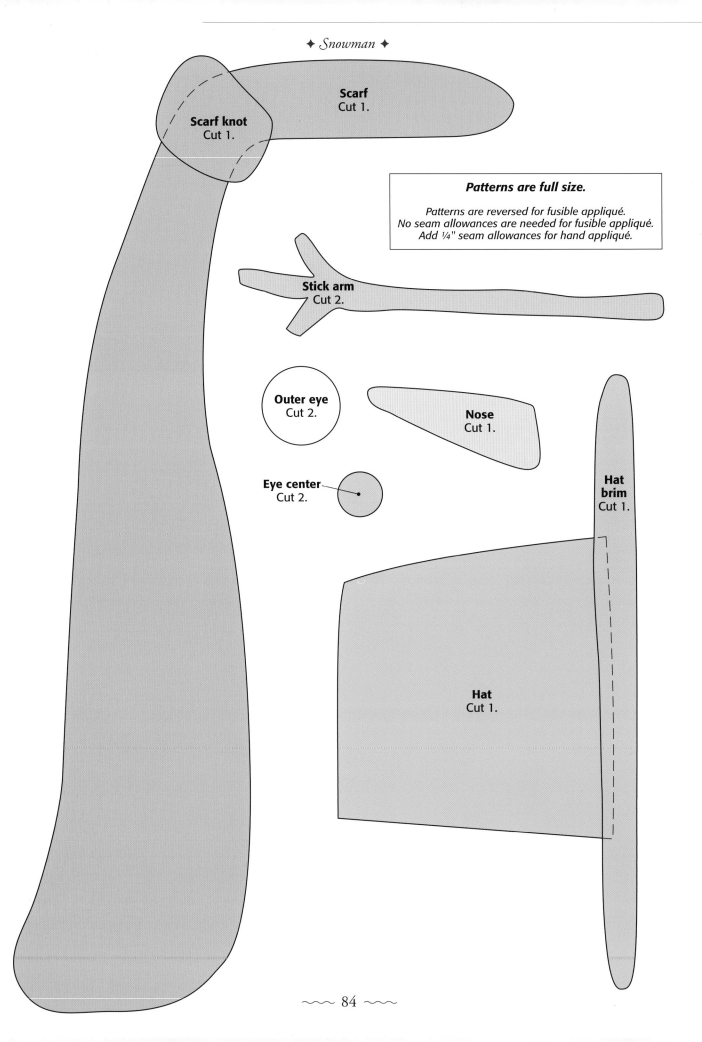

Scarf
Cut 1.

Scarf knot
Cut 1.

Patterns are full size.

Patterns are reversed for fusible appliqué.
No seam allowances are needed for fusible appliqué.
Add ¼" seam allowances for hand appliqué.

Stick arm
Cut 2.

Outer eye
Cut 2.

Nose
Cut 1.

Eye center
Cut 2.

Hat brim
Cut 1.

Hat
Cut 1.

Three Marigolds

Quilt Size: 48" x 41"

The marigold is a colorful addition to any garden. These easy-to-grow and extremely hardy plants evoke special memories for me. My daughter often brought them home to me as a Mother's Day present. The children planted seeds at school in Styrofoam cups, lovingly tended to their plants, and watched them grow. My daughter is grown up now and no longer brings me cups filled with marigolds, but my wish for her is that she will receive cups filled with marigolds from her children.

~Avis

Materials

Yardage is based on 42"-wide fabric.

1⅛ yards of beige print for appliqué background

1 yard of taupe plaid for letter backgrounds

½ yard of mottled gold print for outer marigold petals

⅜ yard of navy print for letters

⅜ yard of gold plaid for inner marigold petals

¼ yard of black print for marigold centers

¼ yard of green #1 for stems

¼ yard of green #2 for leaves

5" square or larger scrap of 16 assorted prints, stripes, and plaids for patchwork

¼ yard of brown print for binding*

2½ yards of backing fabric

47" x 54" piece of batting

*Yardage is sufficient for single-fold binding. Buy ⅜ yard for double-fold binding.

Cutting

Refer to "The Alphabet" on page 11 for cutting the pieces needed for the letters and letter backgrounds.

From the navy print, cut:
✦ Pieces needed for the letters *(THREE MARIGOLDS)*

From the taupe plaid, cut:
✦ Pieces needed for the letter backgrounds *(THREE MARIGOLDS)*
✦ 1 strip, 7½" x 42"; crosscut into 10 sections, 1½" x 7½", and 1 section, 5½" x 7½"
✦ 4 pieces, 1½" x 3½"
✦ 3 strips, 1½" x 42"
✦ 2 strips, 2½" x 32½"

From the beige print, cut:
✦ 3 strips, 11½" x 32½"

From the 16 assorted prints, stripes, and plaids, cut:
✦ 1 square, 4⅞" x 4⅞", from *each* fabric (16 total); cut the squares in half once diagonally to yield 32 triangles

From the brown print, cut:
✦ 5 strips, 1½" x 42"

Piecing the Letters

Piece the letter blocks needed for the words *THREE MARIGOLDS* referring to "The Alphabet" on page 11. Use the navy print for the letters and the taupe plaid for the letter backgrounds. Set the letter units aside.

Appliqué

1. Using the patterns on page 88, prepare three marigold centers, three inner marigold petals, and three outer marigold petals for appliqué. You'll also need to prepare three stems, 1¼" x 19", and nine leaves. We used fusible appliqué and a machine blanket stitch to finish the edges. Refer to "Appliqué" on page 7 for more information.

2. Using your favorite method, appliqué the pieces for each marigold to a 11½" x 32½" beige print strip referring to the photograph on page 85 for placement. Appliqué the stems first; then add the leaves. Add the outer flower petals next so that they overlap the end of the stem. Next appliqué the inner petals followed by the marigold center.

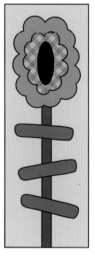

Make 3.

Patchwork

1. Sew the assorted triangles together in pairs to make 16 scrappy triangle squares. Press the seam allowances toward the darker fabric.

Make 16.

2. Sew the triangle squares together into two strips of eight triangle squares each. These completed strips should measure 32½" long.

Make 2.

Assembling the Quilt Top

1. Join the appliqué and triangle-square strips. Press the seam allowances toward the appliqué strips.

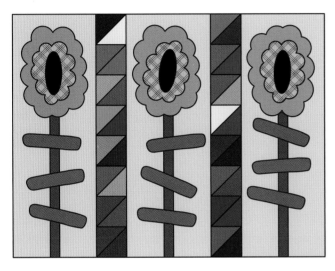

2. Sew the 1½" x 3½" taupe plaid strips to the bottom of the *O, L, D,* and *S* blocks. Then sew these blocks together in a vertical strip. Complete this unit by sewing a 2½" x 32½" taupe plaid strip to each long side. Press all seam allowances toward the taupe strips. Sew this unit to the right side of the quilt top and press the seam allowance toward the appliqué flower.

3. Sew 1½" x 7½" taupe plaid strips to the right side of the *T, H, R, E, M, A, R, I,* and *G* blocks. Sew the 5½" x 7½" taupe plaid rectangle to the right side of the remaining *E* block. Join the letter blocks side by side, making sure the 5½"-wide taupe piece is separating the two words. Add the remaining 1½" x 7½" taupe piece to the left side of this unit. Press all seam allowances toward the pieces.

4. Sew the three 1½" x 42" taupe plaid strips together end to end. From this strip, cut two pieces 48½" long. Sew these strips to the top and bottom of the unit from step 3. Join this row to the top of the quilt. Press the seam allowances toward the taupe plaid strips.

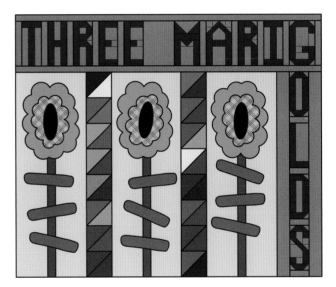

Quilt plan

Finishing

Layer the quilt top, batting, and backing. Baste the layers together and quilt as desired. In the quilt shown, the appliqué shapes were outline quilted by machine and the background was meander quilted. The triangle-square strips were quilted with diagonal lines moving in the opposite direction of the diagonal in each square. Bind the quilt using the 1½" brown print strips, referring to page 9 for more information.

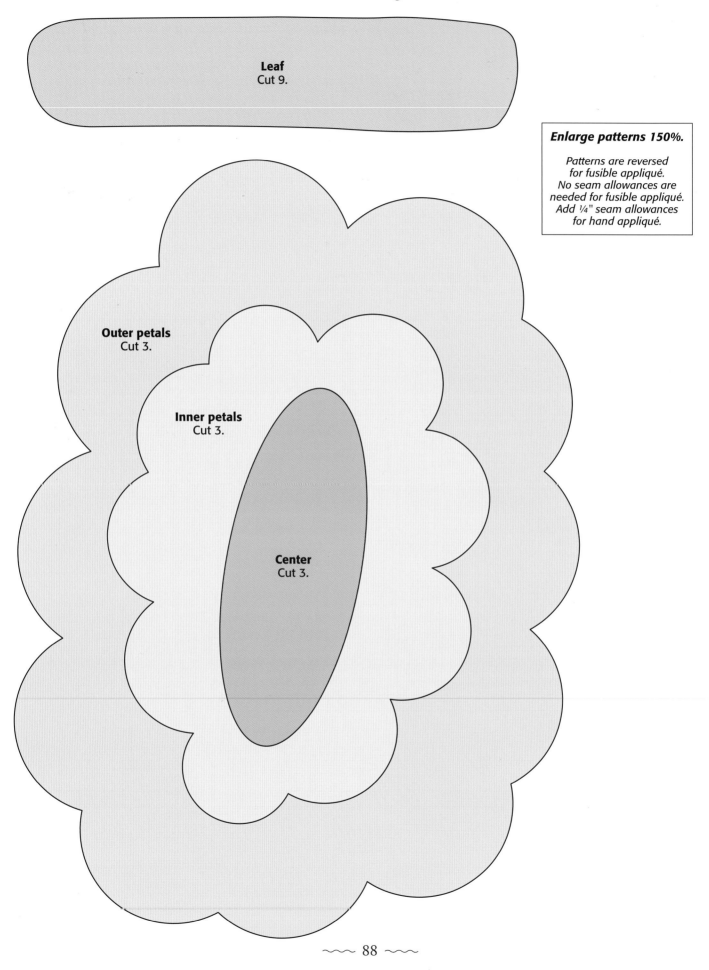

Leaf
Cut 9.

Enlarge patterns 150%.

*Patterns are reversed
for fusible appliqué.
No seam allowances are
needed for fusible appliqué.
Add ¼" seam allowances
for hand appliqué.*

Outer petals
Cut 3.

Inner petals
Cut 3.

Center
Cut 3.

Watering Can

Quilt Size: 45" x 46"

I'm a collector at heart, and watering cans are one of the things I love to collect.
They're great for displaying on benches and tables scattered throughout my backyard.
I have some green ones, a few red ones, and, of course, several galvanized
metal ones. I did not have a blue one—until now!
~Avis

Materials

Yardage is based on 42"-wide fabric.

1⅛ yards of tan print for appliqué background

1 yard of black solid for letters and binding

⅞ yard of pink print for letter backgrounds

⅞ yard of black print for outer border

⅞ yard of blue plaid for watering can

¼ yard of blue print for watering-can accents

¼ yard of green check for leaves

¼ yard of green print for stems

Scraps of 3 dark pinks, 3 light pinks, 1 yellow, and 1 light blue for flower petals, middles, and centers

3¼ yards of backing fabric

51" x 52" piece of batting

Cutting

Refer to "The Alphabet" on page 11 for cutting the pieces needed for the letters and letter backgrounds.

From the black solid, cut:
- ✦ Pieces needed for the letters *(WATERING CAN)*
- ✦ 5 strips, 1½" x 42"*

*If your fabric is not 41½" wide after removing the selvages, you will need to piece strips together to achieve this length.

From the pink print, cut:
- ✦ Pieces needed for the letter backgrounds *(WATERING CAN)*
- ✦ 10 pieces, 1½" x 7½"
- ✦ 2 strips, 1½" x 37½"
- ✦ 3 pieces, 1½" x 4½"
- ✦ 1 piece, 4½" x 5½"
- ✦ 2 strips, 2½" x 29½"

From the tan print, cut:
- ✦ 1 piece, 12½" x 29½"
- ✦ 1 piece, 14½" x 16½"
- ✦ 1 piece, 3½" x 4½"
- ✦ 2 squares, 1½" x 1½"
- ✦ 1 piece, 2½" x 10½"
- ✦ 2 squares, 2½" x 2½"
- ✦ 1 square, 2⅞" x 2⅞"; cut the square in half once diagonally to yield 2 triangles. (Only 1 will be used.)
- ✦ 1 piece, 1½" x 2½"
- ✦ 1 strip, 1½" x 13½"

From the blue plaid, cut:
- ✦ 1 piece, 11½" x 16½"
- ✦ 1 piece, 1½" x 2½"
- ✦ 1 strip, 1½" x 11½"
- ✦ 1 square, 1½" x 1½"
- ✦ 1 square, 2½" x 2½"
- ✦ 1 square, 2⅞" x 2⅞"; cut the square in half once diagonally to yield 2 triangles. (Only 1 will be used.)

From the black print, cut:
- ✦ 5 strips, 4½" x 42"

Piecing the Letters

Piece the letter blocks needed for the words *WATERING CAN* referring to "The Alphabet" on page 11. Use the black solid for the letters and the pink print for the letter backgrounds.

1. Sew the letters for the *WATERING* unit together, alternating them with seven 1½" x 7½" pink print strips. Sew one of these pink strips to each end of the unit. Sew the 1½" x 37½" pink strips to the top and bottom of the unit. Press all seam allowances toward the pink strips.

2. Sew the remaining 1½" x 7½" pink strip to the right of the *C* block. Then sew a 1½" x 4½" pink print strip to the bottom of the *C, A,* and *N* blocks. Join the letters vertically. Sew the 4½" x 5½" pink piece to the top of this unit. Then join the two 2½" x 29½" pink strips to the sides. Press all seam allowances toward the pink strips.

Constructing the Watering Can

1. Using the blue print fabric, cut two bias strips, 1⅜" x 14". Make two bias tubes referring to "Making Bias Vines" on page 9. Appliqué the tubes onto the blue plaid rectangle, referring to the photo on page 89 for placement.

    Using the folded-corner technique on page 7, sew the 2½" tan print squares to adjacent corners on the short end of the 11½" x 16½" blue plaid piece. Then join this to the right side of the 14½" x 16½" tan print piece. Set aside.

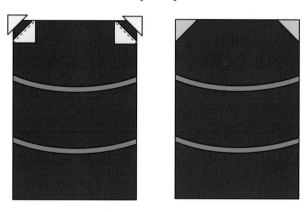

2. To make the watering-can handle, use the folded-corner technique to join the 1½" blue plaid square to the top-right corner of the 2½" x 10½" tan print strip. Sew the 2½" blue plaid square to the bottom-right corner in the same manner.

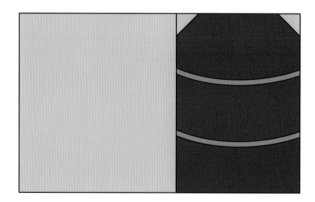

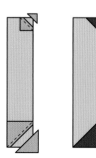

3. Sew the 2⅞" blue plaid and tan triangles together to form a triangle square. Sew this to the bottom of the unit from step 2. Sew the 1½" x 2½" blue plaid piece to the top of this unit.

4. Sew the 1½" tan print squares to the top and bottom of the 1½" x 11½" blue plaid strip using the folded-corner technique. Make sure the pieces are angled as shown. Add the 1½" x 2½" tan print piece to the bottom of this unit.

5. Join the two handle sections and then add the 1½" x 13½" tan strip to the right side of the unit. Sew the 3½" x 4½" tan piece to the top of this unit to complete the handle.

6. Add the handle to the right side of the unit from step 1 on page 91. Join the 12½" x 29½" tan piece to the top of the watering can and the 1½" x 29½" tan strip to the bottom. Attach the *CAN* unit to the right side of the watering-can unit. Then sew the *WATERING* unit to the top.

Appliqué

1. Using the patterns on pages 93 and 94, prepare the flowers, leaves, and watering-can spout for fusible appliqué referring to "Appliqué" on page 7 for instructions.

2. Referring to the quilt photograph on page 89 for placement help, appliqué the spout onto the background fabric to the left side of the pieced watering can. Add a blue accent piece to the spout referring to step 1 on page 91. We used a machine blanket stitch around these pieces to add a decorative touch. Add the leaves next and stitch around them with a blanket stitch before positioning the stems on top of them.

3. To make the stems, prepare a bias vine, ½" x 35", referring to "Making Bias Vines." Cut the long bias tube into the following lengths, which will be positioned in order from left to right: 5", 9", 6", 9", and 3½". Stitch the stems in place by hand or by machine using a blind hem stitch and matching thread.

4. Add the three large outer petals, the middle layer, and finally the small flower centers. We used a machine blanket stitch around each layer of the flower pieces. Appliqué the smaller blue flowers in the same manner.

Adding the Borders

1. Trim two of the 4½" black print strips to 37½" long and sew to the top and bottom of the quilt. Press the seam allowance toward the black strips.

2. Sew the three remaining 4½" black print strips together end to end to create one long strip. From this strip, cut two pieces 4½" x 46½" and sew them to the sides of the quilt. Press the seam allowances toward the black strips.

Quilt plan

Finishing

Layer the quilt top, batting, and backing. Baste the layers together and quilt as desired. In the quilt shown, the watering can, flowers, and letters were outline quilted by machine and then the background was meander quilted. The watering can was quilted with diagonal lines in the upper third of the can and also in the spout. The remainder of the watering can was quilted by following the plaid design. Bind the quilt using the 1½" black solid strips referring to page 9 for more information.

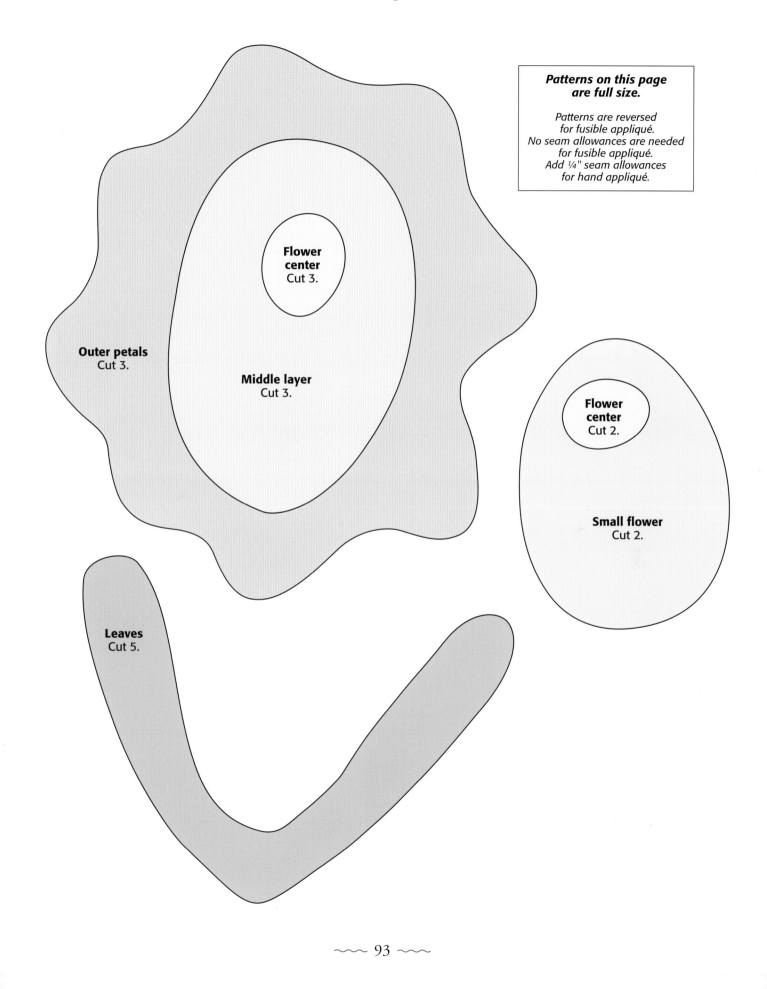

Flower center
Cut 3.

Outer petals
Cut 3.

Middle layer
Cut 3.

Patterns on this page are full size.

Patterns are reversed for fusible appliqué. No seam allowances are needed for fusible appliqué. Add ¼" seam allowances for hand appliqué.

Flower center
Cut 2.

Small flower
Cut 2.

Leaves
Cut 5.

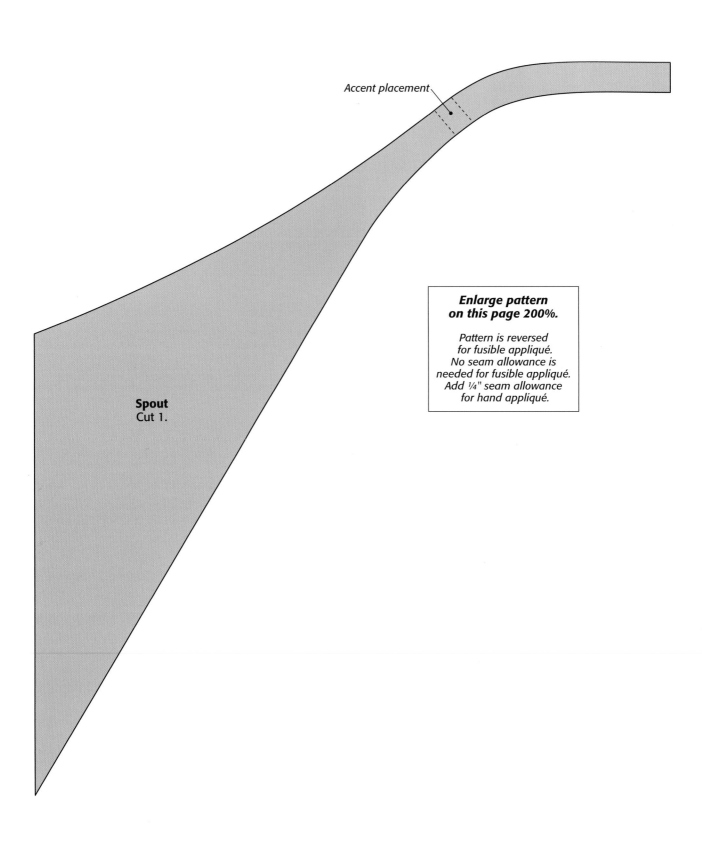

Accent placement

Spout
Cut 1.

**Enlarge pattern
on this page 200%.**

*Pattern is reversed
for fusible appliqué.
No seam allowance is
needed for fusible appliqué.
Add ¼" seam allowance
for hand appliqué.*

Wool

Quilt Size: 43" x 32"

*Wool is one of our favorite things. We love to work with wool whether we're
rug hooking, stitching penny rugs, or just adding touches of it to our quilts. The rich
texture and wonderful colors of hand-dyed wool add dimension and interest to any project.
~ Tammy*

Materials

Yardage is based on 42"-wide fabric.

¾ yard of medium brown print for outer border and binding

⅝ yard of tan stripe for willow tree and flying-geese backgrounds

⅜ yard of tan check for sheep background

⅜ yard of tan print for letter backgrounds

Fat quarter of green wool or cotton for willow tree branches

¼ yard of cream solid for sheep

¼ yard of dark brown print for letters

¼ yard of brown-and-red stripe for inner border

¼ yard or scraps of gold wool or cotton for stars

⅛ yard of green print for ground under sheep

⅛ yard *each* of 8 assorted darks for flying-geese strip

⅛ yard or scrap of black stripe for sheep heads and legs

⅛ yard or scrap of black solid for sheep ears and tails

⅛ yard of brown wool or cotton for tree trunk

1⅝ yards of backing fabric

38" x 50" piece of batting

Optional: Brown, green, and gold embroidery floss or pearl cotton for appliquéing the wool by hand

Cutting

Refer to "The Alphabet" on page 11 for cutting the pieces needed for the letters and letter backgrounds.

From the dark brown print, cut:
✦ Pieces needed for the letters *(WOOL)*

From the tan print, cut:
✦ Pieces needed for the letter backgrounds *(WOOL)*
✦ 3 pieces, 1½" x 7½"
✦ 1 strip, 3½" x 22½"

From the tan check, cut:
✦ 1 piece, 8½" x 16½"
✦ 1 piece, 4½" x 5½"
✦ 1 square, 2½" x 2½"
✦ 12 squares, 1½" x 1½"
✦ 4 pieces, 1" x 1½"

From the cream solid, cut:
✦ 2 squares, 6½" x 6½"

From the black stripe, cut:
✦ 2 pieces, 1½" x 2½"
✦ 8 pieces, 1" x 1½"

From the assorted dark prints, cut:
✦ 8 pieces, 3½" x 6½" (one from each print)

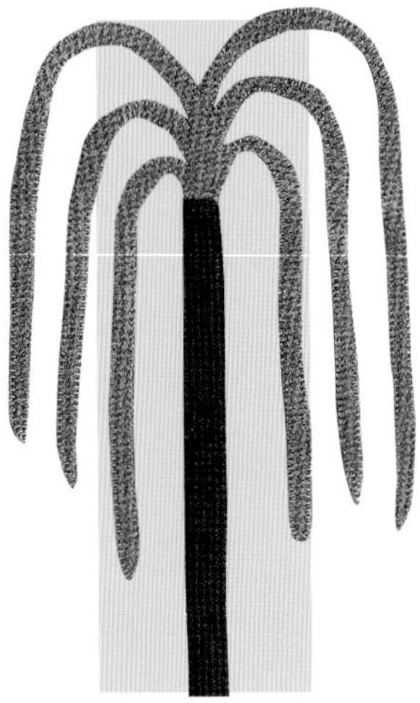

From the tan stripe, cut:
✦ 16 squares, 3½" x 3½"
✦ 1 piece, 10½" x 22½"

From the green print, cut:
✦ 1 strip, 2½" x 29½"

From the brown-and-red stripe, cut:
✦ 2 strips, 1½" x 35½"
✦ 2 strips, 1½" x 26½"

From the medium brown print, cut:
✦ 2 strips, 3½" x 37½"
✦ 2 strips, 3½" x 32½"
✦ 4 strips, 1½" x 42" (for *single-fold* binding)

From the brown wool, cut:
✦ 1 strip, ⅞" x 14½"

Piecing the Letters

1. Piece the letter blocks needed for the word *WOOL* referring to "The Alphabet" on page 11. Use the dark brown print for the letters and the tan print for the letter backgrounds.

2. Stitch the three 1½" x 7½" tan print pieces between the letters as shown.

Constructing the Sheep Unit

1. Piece together three 1½" tan check squares, two 1" x 1½" tan check pieces, and four 1" x 1½" black stripe pieces as shown to make a leg unit for the sheep. Repeat to make two of these units.

Make 2.

2. Using the folded-corner technique on page 7, sew 1½" tan check squares to adjacent corners of a 6½" cream square. Repeat to make two of these sheep bodies. Sew the leg units from step 1 to the bottom of these units.

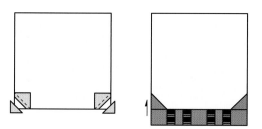

3. Using the folded-corner technique, stitch a 1½" tan check square to a 1½" x 2½" black stripe piece as shown. Repeat to make a second unit, but change the stitching angle as shown. Press the seam allowances toward the black stripe.

Make 1 of each.

4. Stitch the two units from step 3 to both sides of the 2½" tan check square. Then sew the 4½" x 5½" tan check piece to the bottom of this unit.

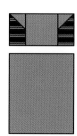

5. Sew the sheep-body units from step 2 to the sides of the unit from step 4. Add the 8½" x 16½" tan check rectangle to the top.

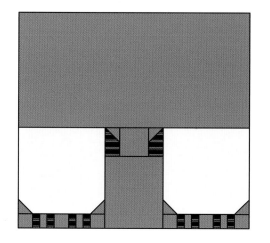

Constructing the Flying-Geese Strip

1. Using the folded-corner technique, stitch 3½" tan stripe squares to opposite corners of the eight dark print rectangles. Stitch diagonally, trim, and press.

Make 8.

2. Stitch the flying-geese units together in a vertical column. Press all seam allowances in one direction.

Assembling the Quilt Top

1. Stitch the *WOOL* unit to the top of the sheep unit. Then stitch the 10½" x 22½" tan stripe rectangle to the left of the sheep and the 3½" x 22½" tan print strip to the right. Press the seam allowances toward the tan pieces.

2. Join the 2½" x 29½" green print strip to the bottom of the unit. Attach the flying-geese strip to the right side.

3. Sew the 1½" x 35½" brown-and-red stripe strips to the top and bottom of the quilt top. Sew the 1½" x 26½" brown-and-red stripe strips to the sides of the quilt. Press all seam allowances toward the striped borders.

4. Sew the 3½" x 37½" medium brown print strips to the top and bottom of the quilt top. Sew the 3½" x 32½" medium brown print strips to the sides of the quilt. Press all seam allowances toward the medium brown strips.

Appliqué

1. Using the patterns on pages 98 and 99, prepare the willow branches (one piece), sheep tails and ears, and three stars for fusible appliqué referring to "Appliqué" on page 7 for instructions. The brown ⅞" x 14½" strip is for the tree trunk. We used wool for the willow tree and stars, but cotton would work fine too.

2. Appliqué an ear and a tail onto each of the sheep. Appliqué three stars above the sheep. Next appliqué the willow branches. Then appliqué the trunk. We fused each piece in place and stitched around them with a machine blanket stitch. If you're using wool for your appliqué, you can stitch them by machine or by hand using pearl cotton or embroidery floss.

Finishing

Layer the quilt top, batting, and backing. Baste the layers together and quilt as desired. In the quilt shown, the background was machine quilted with a small stipple pattern. The sheep were quilted with a loopy stipple. The letters and flying-geese strip were quilted in the ditch. Then an upside-down flying-geese shape was quilted in the pieced flying-geese strip to form a diamond grid. Triangles were quilted in the outer border. Bind the quilt using the 1½" medium brown print strips, referring to page 9 for more information.

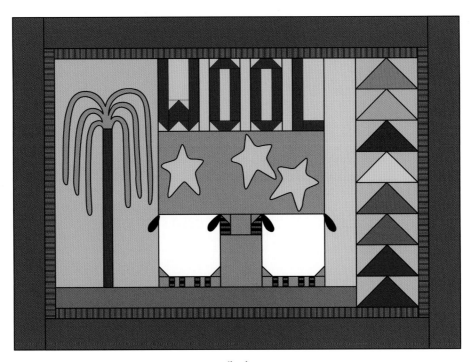

Quilt plan

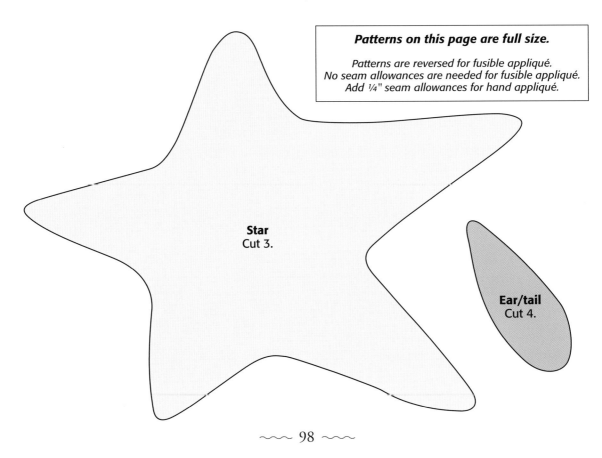

Patterns on this page are full size.

Patterns are reversed for fusible appliqué.
No seam allowances are needed for fusible appliqué.
Add ¼" seam allowances for hand appliqué.

Star
Cut 3.

Ear/tail
Cut 4.

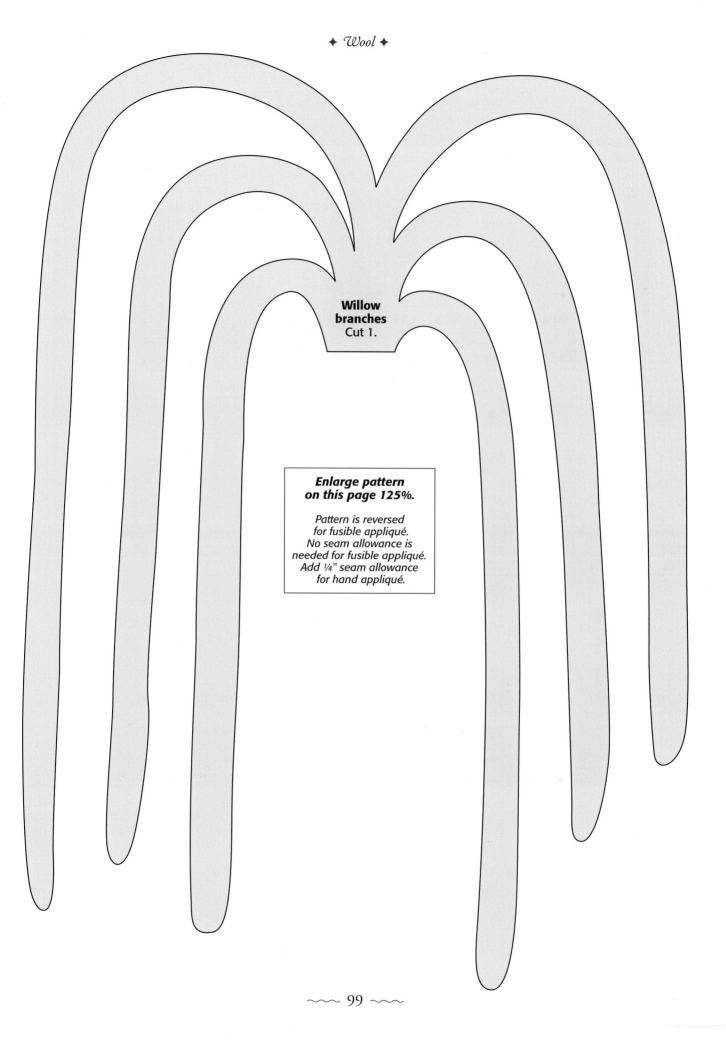

**Willow
branches**
Cut 1.

***Enlarge pattern
on this page 125%.***

*Pattern is reversed
for fusible appliqué.
No seam allowance is
needed for fusible appliqué.
Add ¼" seam allowance
for hand appliqué.*

Alphabet Sampler

Quilt Size: 46" x 54"

This quilt was very fun to make. In addition to using all the letters of the alphabet, it includes a wide variety of fabrics. This would be a great quilt to hang anywhere, but this one is for my first grandchild's bedroom. I think it will be a lovely addition to the room and a fun way for a growing child to learn the alphabet!
~Avis

Materials

Yardage is based on 42"-wide fabric.

1 yard of brown print for outer border

½ yard *each* of 8 assorted light prints, plaids, and strips for appliqué backgrounds

⅜ yard *each* of 3 assorted reds for ladybug, watermelon, and heart

⅜ yard of black print #1 for inner border

⅜ yard of brown plaid for basket

⅜ yard of black solid for cat and ladybug

⅜ yard of purple for star

¼ yard *each* of 13 assorted light prints, plaids, and stripes (#1–#13) for letter backgrounds

¼ yard *each* of 26 assorted dark prints, plaids, and stripes for letters

¼ yard of orange for pumpkin

¼ yard of green for watermelon rind

¼ yard of light fabric for watermelon rind

Scraps of 3 assorted pinks for flower and cat nose

Scrap of green check for pumpkin stem appliqués

⅜ yard of black print #2 for binding*

4 yards of backing fabric

52" x 60" piece of batting

Two ½"-diameter buttons for cat eyes

1 package of white baby rickrack

1 bottle of Rit black fabric dye for rickrack

*Yardage is sufficient for single-fold binding. Buy ½ yard for double-fold binding.

Cutting

Refer to "The Alphabet" on page 11 for cutting the pieces needed for the letters and letter backgrounds.

From the 8 assorted light fabrics for appliqué backgrounds, cut:
- 1 piece, 9½" x 12½"
- 3 squares, 9½" x 9½"
- 2 pieces, 7½" x 9½"
- 1 piece, 6½" x 9½"
- 1 piece, 5½" x 9½"

From *each* of the 26 dark prints, plaids, and stripes for letters, cut:
- Pieces needed for *one* letter of the alphabet

From light #1, cut:
- Background pieces needed for the letters *A* and *B*
- 3 pieces, 1½" x 7½"
- 2 pieces, 1½" x 10½"

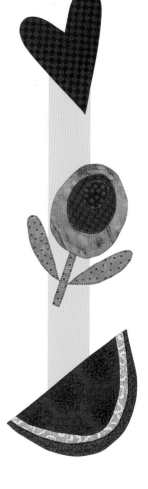

From light #2, cut:
- Background pieces needed for the letter *C*
- 2 pieces, 1½" x 7½"
- 2 pieces, 1½" x 5½"

From light #3, cut:
- Background pieces needed for the letter *D*
- 2 pieces, 1½" x 7½"
- 2 pieces, 1½" x 5½"

From light #4, cut:
- Background pieces needed for the letters *E* and *F*
- 3 pieces, 1½" x 7½"
- 2 pieces, 1½" x 9½"

From light #5, cut:
- Background pieces needed for the letters *G* and *H*
- 3 pieces, 1½" x 7½"
- 2 pieces, 1½" x 10½"

From light #6, cut:
- Background pieces needed for the letter *I*
- 2 pieces, 1½" x 7½"
- 2 pieces, 1½" x 5½"

From light #7, cut:
- Background pieces needed for the letters *J, K,* and *L*
- 4 pieces, 1½" x 7½"
- 2 pieces, 1½" x 14½"

From light #8, cut:
- Background pieces needed for the letters *M, N,* and *O*
- 4 pieces, 1½" x 7½"
- 2 pieces, 1½" x 15½"

From light #9, cut:
- Background pieces needed for the letter *P*
- 2 pieces, 1½" x 7½"
- 2 pieces, 1½" x 5½"

From light #10, cut:
- Background pieces needed for the letters *Q, R,* and *S*
- 4 pieces, 1½" x 7½"
- 2 pieces, 1½" x 13½"

From light #11, cut:
- ◆ Background pieces needed for the letters *T* and *U*
- ◆ 3 pieces, 1½" x 7½"
- ◆ 2 pieces, 1½" x 9½"

From light #12, cut:
- ◆ Background pieces needed for the letters *V* and *W*
- ◆ 3 pieces, 1½" x 7½"
- ◆ 2 pieces, 1½" x 11½"

From light #13, cut:
- ◆ Background pieces needed for the letters *X, Y,* and *Z*
- ◆ 4 pieces, 1½" x 7½"
- ◆ 2 pieces, 1½" x 15½"

From black print #1, cut:
- ◆ 5 strips, 1½" x 42"

From the brown print, cut:
- ◆ 5 strips, 3½" x 42"

From black print #2, cut:
- ◆ 6 strips, 1½" x 42" (for *single-fold* binding)

Appliqué

Using the patterns on pages 105–112, prepare and appliqué the pieces for the basket, cat, flower, heart, ladybug, pumpkin, and watermelon. We used fusible appliqué and then machine blanket-stitched around each shape.

1. Use the following light fabric pieces for the appliqué backgrounds:
   - The three 9½" squares for the basket, cat, and ladybug
   - The two 7½" x 9½" rectangles for the flower and heart
   - The 5½" x 9½" rectangle for the pumpkin
   - The 6½" x 9½" rectangle for the star
   - The 9½" x 12½" rectangle for the watermelon

2. Cut and fuse a ⅜" x 8½" black solid strip down the middle of the ladybug's back. Placement is indicated with dotted lines on the pattern.

3. Cut and fuse a ½" x 3½" green stem for the flower block.

4. The cat has hand-dyed gray rickrack whiskers. (Refer to "Dye Your Own Rickrack" below.) Cut the rickrack into three 5"-long pieces. Place the rickrack referring to the quilt photograph on page 100 and stitch it in place with a very narrow zigzag stitch; then appliqué the cat's nose on top of the crisscrossed rickrack pieces.

Dye Your Own Rickrack

Using a glass measuring cup, add approximately 2 tablespoons of black dye to ½ cup of water. Stir well. Moisten the rickrack and then add it to the dye solution. Cook in the microwave for approximately one minute. Check the color. If it is too light, continue cooking at one-minute intervals until the right shade is achieved. Rinse well and dry. The desired color is a soft to medium shade of gray. Please note: *Do not* use this measuring cup for any food preparation. Keep it for dyeing purposes only.

Piecing the Letters

The alphabet is divided into 13 units, with each unit sharing the same light background fabric. Referring to the cutting list on page 101 and at left, select the appropriate background pieces and additional spacer pieces for each letter or group of letters. Piece the letter blocks referring to "The Alphabet" on page 11. Then join the letters into the 13 units as described below. Press all seam allowances toward the background pieces.

1. Join the *A* and *B* blocks and the three 1½" x 7½" light #1 strips as shown. Sew the two 1½" x 10½" light #1 strips to the top and bottom of the unit.

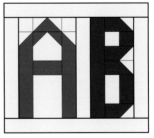

2. Sew a 1½" x 7½" light #2 strip to each side of the *C* block. Then add the two 1½" x 5½" light #2 strips to the top and bottom of the block. Prepare the *D* block in the same manner using light #3 strips. *Do not* sew these blocks together.

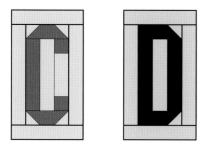

3. Join the *E* and *F* blocks with the three 1½" x 7½" light #4 strips as shown. Sew the two 1½" x 9½" light #4 strips to the top and bottom of the unit.

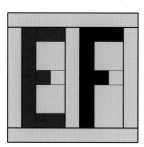

4. Join the *G* and *H* blocks with the three 1½" x 7½" light #5 strips as shown. Then sew the two 1½" x 10½" light #5 strips to the top and bottom of the unit.

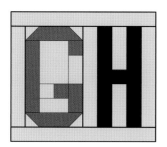

5. Sew a 1½" x 7½" light #6 strip to each side of the *I* block. Sew the two 1½" x 5½" light #6 strips to the top and bottom of the block.

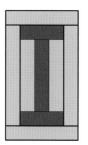

6. Join the *J, K,* and *L* blocks, alternating them with the four 1½" x 7½" light #7 strips as shown. Then sew the two 1½" x 14½" light #7 strips to the top and bottom of the unit. Prepare the *MNO* unit in the same manner, using the 1½" x 7½" and 1½" x 15½" light #8 strips.

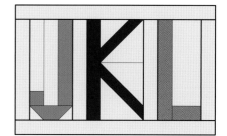

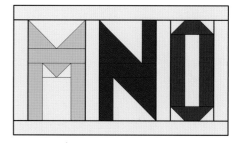

7. Sew a 1½" x 7½" light #9 strip to each side of the *P* block. Sew the two 1½" x 5½" light #9 strips to the top and bottom of the block.

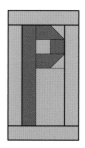

8. Join the *Q, R,* and *S* blocks with the four 1½" x 7½" light #10 strips as shown. Sew the two 1½" x 13½" light #10 strips to the top and bottom of the unit.

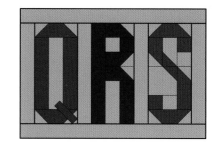

9. Join the *T* and *U* blocks and the three 1½" x 7½" light #11 strips as shown. Then sew the two 1½" x 9½" light #11 strips to the top and bottom of the unit.

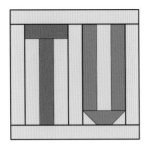

10. Join the *V* and *W* blocks and the three 1½" x 7½" light #12 strips as shown. Sew the two 1½" x 11½" light #12 strips to the top and bottom of the unit.

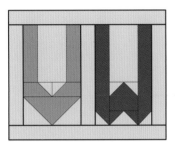

11. Join the *X, Y,* and *Z* blocks with the four 1½" x 7½" light #13 strips as shown. Then sew the two 1½" x 15½" light #13 strips to the top and bottom of the unit.

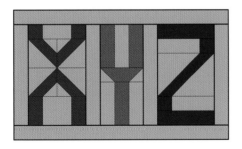

Assembling the Quilt Top

1. Sew the letter sections and the appliquéd blocks together into rows referring to the quilt plan at right. Sew the rows together and press the seam allowances in one direction.

2. Trim two of the 1½" black print #1 strips to 38½" long and sew them to the top and bottom of the quilt. Sew the remaining three black #1 strips together end to end. From this long strip, cut two strips 1½" x 47½" and sew them to the sides of the quilt. Press all seam allowances toward the black borders.

3. Trim two of the 3½" brown print strips to 40½" long and sew them to the top and bottom of the quilt. Sew the remaining three brown strips together end to end. From this long strip, cut two strips 3½" x 53½" and sew them to the sides of the quilt. Press all seam allowances toward the brown print borders.

Quilt plan

Finishing

Layer the quilt top, batting, and backing. Baste the layers together and quilt as desired. In the quilt shown, the background was machine quilted with a meandering pattern and a double row of hearts was quilted in the outer border. Stitch the buttons in place for the cat's eyes. Bind the quilt using the 1½" black print #2 strips, referring to page 9 for more information.

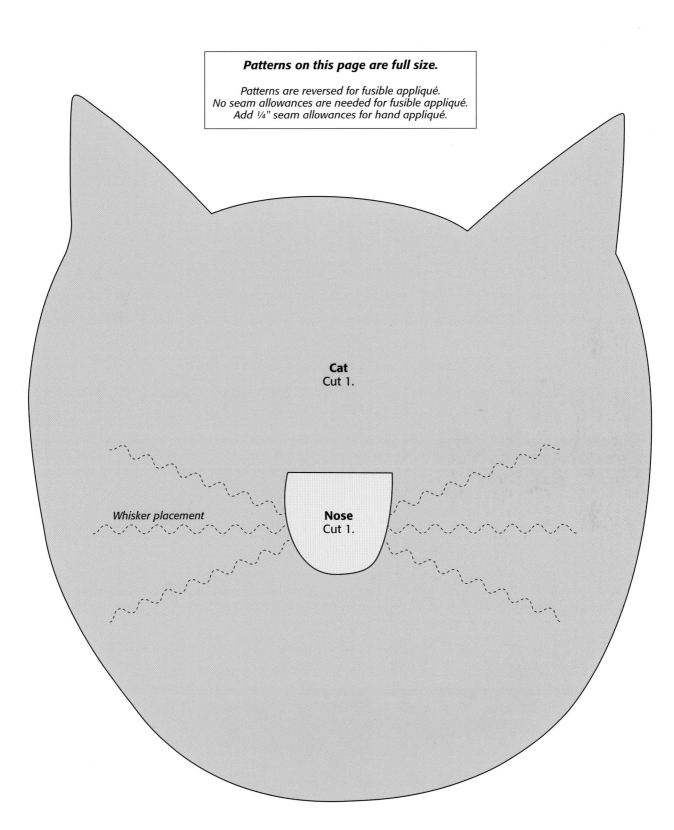

Patterns on this page are full size.

Patterns are reversed for fusible appliqué.
No seam allowances are needed for fusible appliqué.
Add ¼" seam allowances for hand appliqué.

Cat
Cut 1.

Whisker placement

Nose
Cut 1.

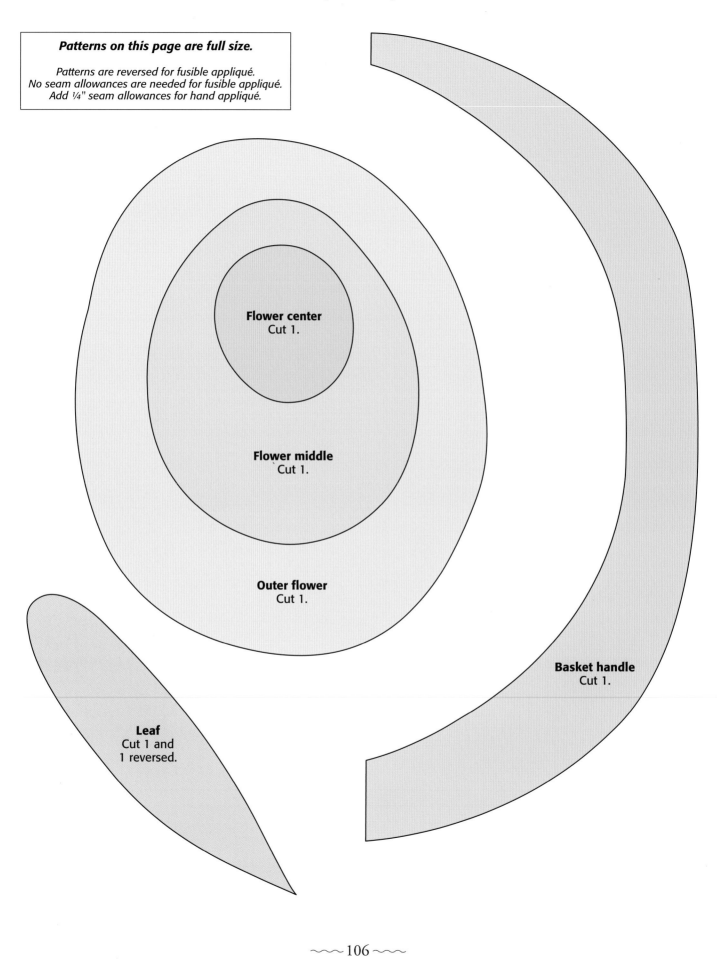

Patterns on this page are full size.

Patterns are reversed for fusible appliqué.
No seam allowances are needed for fusible appliqué.
Add ¼" seam allowances for hand appliqué.

Flower center
Cut 1.

Flower middle
Cut 1.

Outer flower
Cut 1.

Basket handle
Cut 1.

Leaf
Cut 1 and
1 reversed.

Pattern on this page is full size.

Pattern is reversed for fusible appliqué.
No seam allowance is needed for fusible appliqué.
Add ¼" seam allowance for hand appliqué.

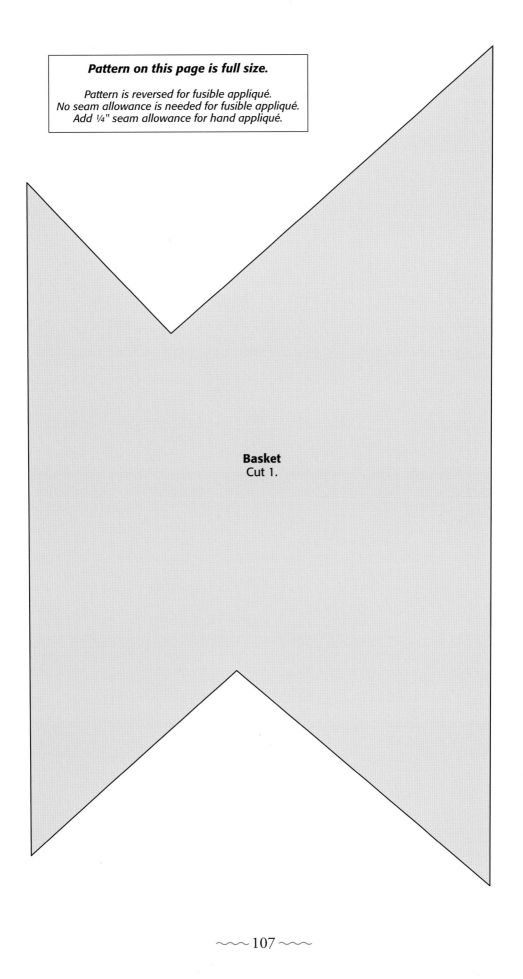

Basket
Cut 1.

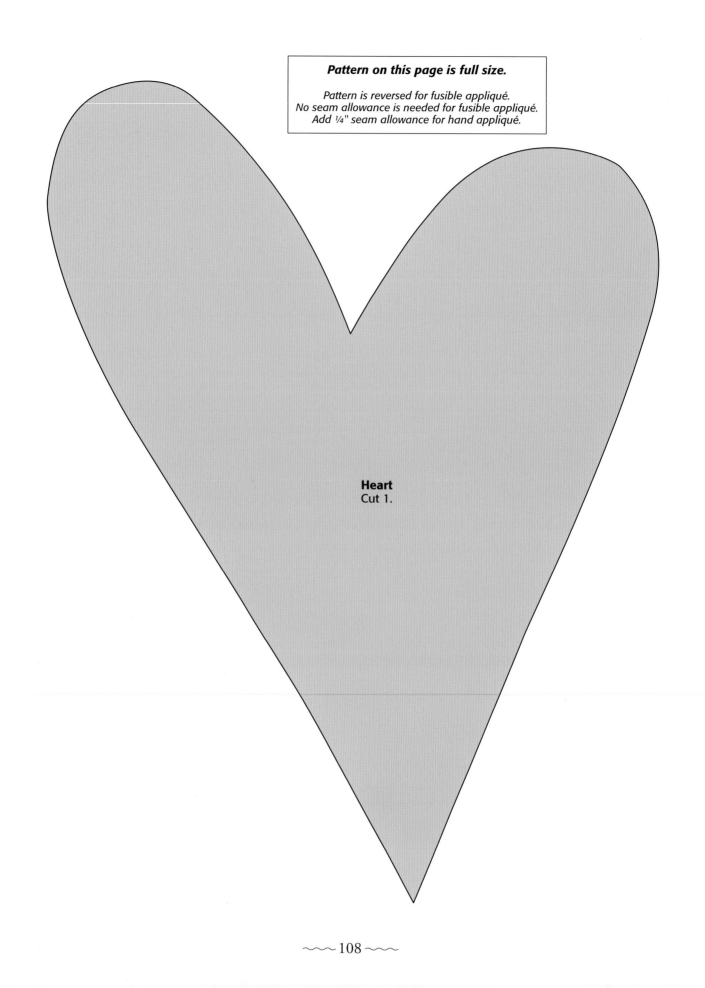

Pattern on this page is full size.

Pattern is reversed for fusible appliqué.
No seam allowance is needed for fusible appliqué.
Add ¼" seam allowance for hand appliqué.

Heart
Cut 1.

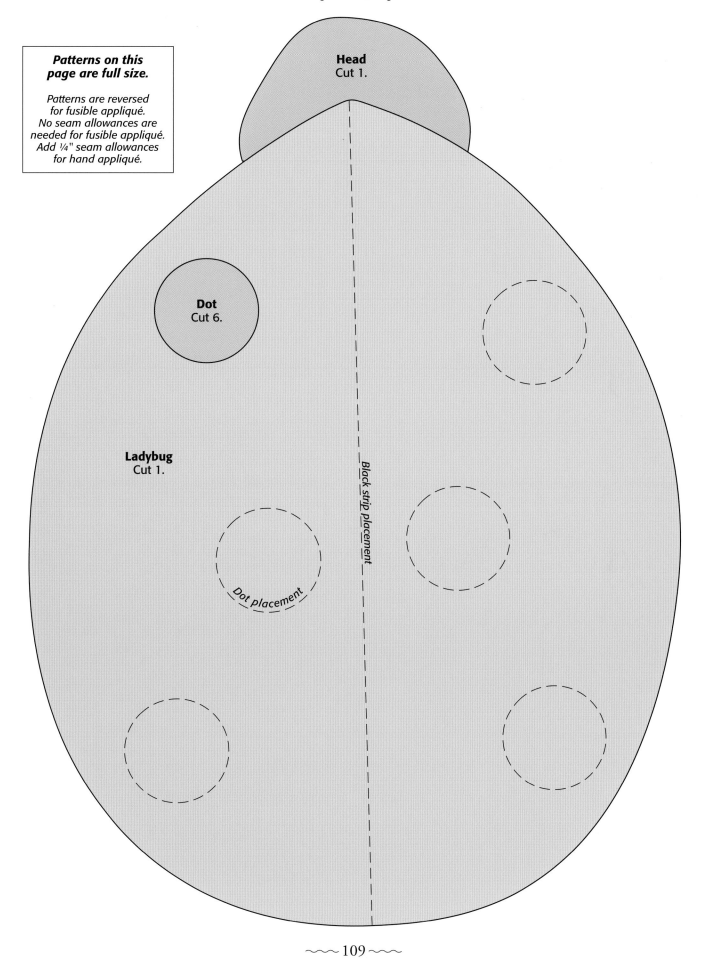

Patterns on this page are full size.

Patterns are reversed for fusible appliqué. No seam allowances are needed for fusible appliqué. Add ¼" seam allowances for hand appliqué.

Head
Cut 1.

Dot
Cut 6.

Ladybug
Cut 1.

Black strip placement

Dot placement

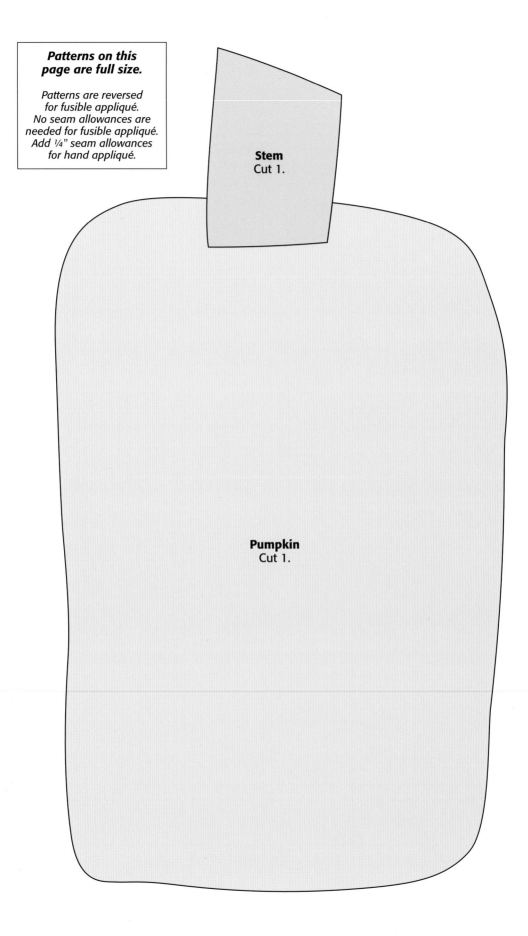

Patterns on this page are full size.

*Patterns are reversed
for fusible appliqué.
No seam allowances are
needed for fusible appliqué.
Add ¼" seam allowances
for hand appliqué.*

Stem
Cut 1.

Pumpkin
Cut 1.

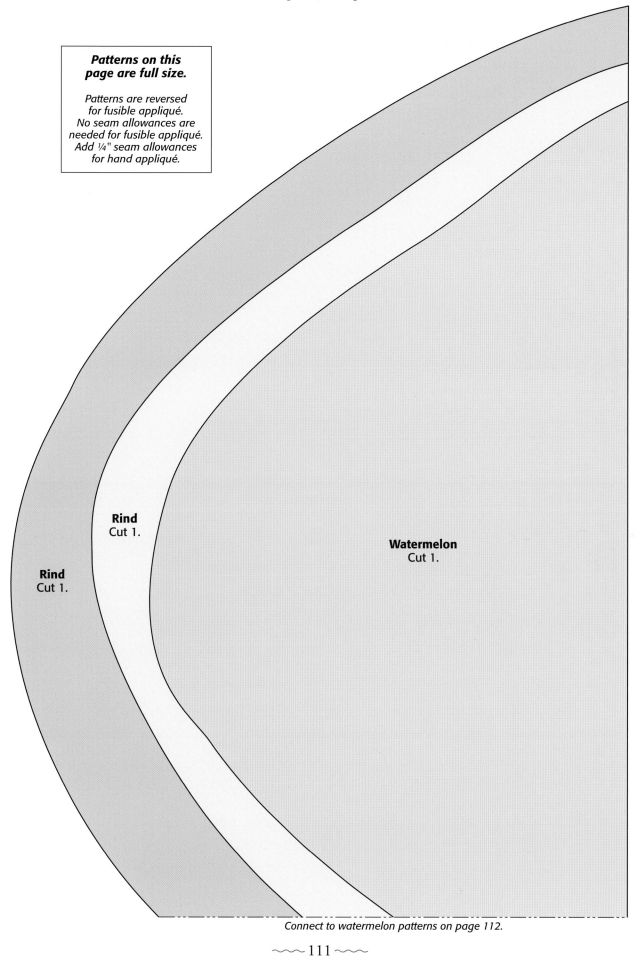

Patterns on this page are full size.

Patterns are reversed for fusible appliqué. No seam allowances are needed for fusible appliqué. Add ¼" seam allowances for hand appliqué.

Rind
Cut 1.

Rind
Cut 1.

Watermelon
Cut 1.

Connect to watermelon patterns on page 112.

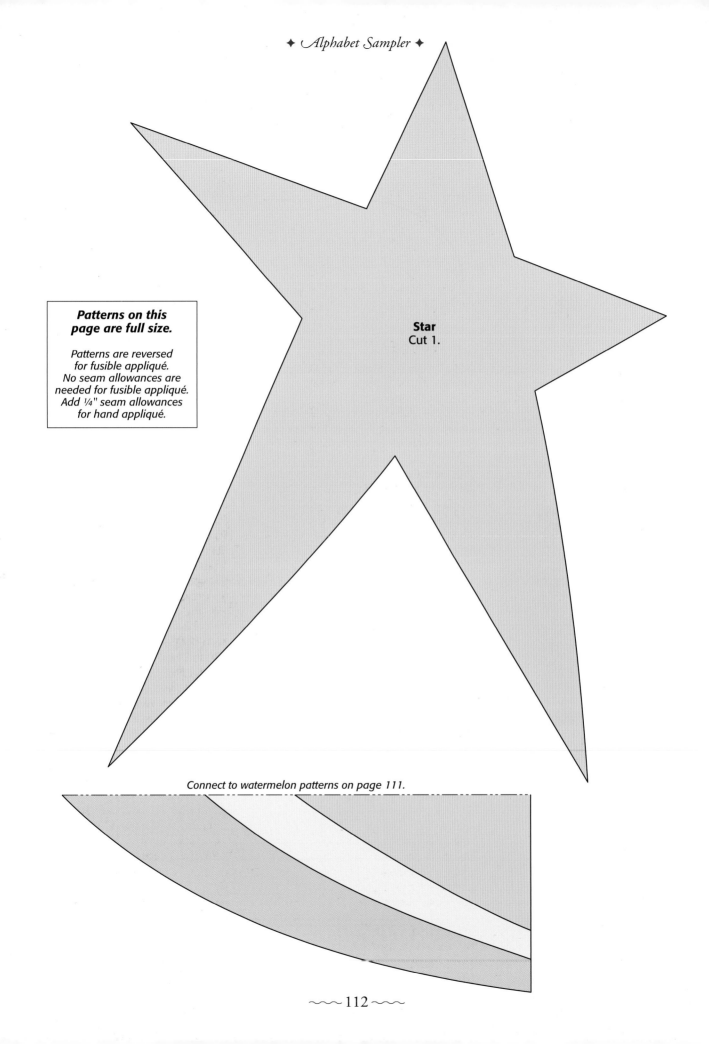

Patterns on this page are full size.

*Patterns are reversed
for fusible appliqué.
No seam allowances are
needed for fusible appliqué.
Add ¼" seam allowances
for hand appliqué.*

Star
Cut 1.

Connect to watermelon patterns on page 111.